A LIBERIAN SOCIAL WORKER IN ENGLAND

Reflections on the Glass Ceiling

James Martin Johnson

Mereo Books

2nd Floor, 6-8 Dyer Street, Cirencester, Gloucestershire, GL7 2PF
An imprint of Memoirs Books. www.mereobooks.com
and www.memoirsbooks.co.uk

Reflections on the glass ceiling

978-1-86151-349-6

First published in Great Britain in 2021
by Mereo Books, an imprint of Memoirs Books.

The address for Memoirs Books can be
found at www.mereobooks.com

Mereo Books Ltd. Reg. No. 12157152

Typeset in 11/15pt Century Schoolbook
by Wiltshire Associates.
Printed and bound in Great Britain

Dedication

Reflections on the Glass Ceiling is dedicated to Karen, the rainbow in my cloud.

Contents

Part 4

CARVING OUT MY NICHE

Part 5

MY WILDERNESS YEAR

Part 6

EMBRACING THE NEW: LIFE BEYOND SOCIAL SERVICES

Part 7

THE BLACK PROFESSIONAL

Chronology/Timeline
Bibliography

Note to readers

TO PROTECT THE PRIVACY AND CONFIDENTIALITY of the clients and professionals with whom I worked during my 25 years with East Sussex Social Services, I have made some changes to the book. Nobody's real name has been used.

Acknowledgements

With love and gratitude to my wife, Karen, who was an essential part of my journey from England to America, then to Liberia and back to England.

Love to my son, Michael, and daughter, Michelle, who sadly did not experience the Liberian dream due to the military coup and civil unrest. I am proud of their success and achievements.

To my four grandchildren, Theo, Olivia, Jacob and Solomon, who have brought so much joy and enrichment to the family.

A number of other people have also made valuable contributions to this book. My thanks and appreciation to Martin Jones for his valuable time spent providing feedback on my typescript. Thanks to Erica Smith for her professional advice and guidance. My appreciation to the author Ann Kramer for her advice and guidance. To Jem Price, University of Brighton, for his advice and guidance.

To my African friend and author Alex Mvuka Ntung for his advice. To Marc Turczanski for his assistance in proofreading.

My gratitude and appreciation to all my friends and social work colleagues who have encouraged me to complete this book.

Many thanks to my editor, Aruna Vasudevan, for her understanding, advice and guidance in helping to shape this book into something that would make my family proud.

List of Acronyms

AASW ....Advanced Award in Social Work

ACS ....American Colonisation Society

AMP ....Approved mental health professional

ASW ....Approved social worker

CBT..............Cognitive behaviour therapy

CMHT ....Community mental health teams (UK)

CSM ....Community services manager

CCETSW .....Central Council for Education and
Training in Social Work, UK

CSS ....Certificate in Social Service (UK)

EBP...............Evidence-Based Practice

ELWA ....Eternal Love Winning Africa
(radio station, Liberia)

HIV/AIDS.....Human immunodeficiency
virus/acquired immune deficiency syndrome

LEC..............Liberian Electricity Corporation

NHS ....National Health Service (UK)

OIC ....Officer-in-charge

PAL ....Progressive Alliance of Liberia

PE ....Practice educator

PRC..............People's Redemption Council

Preface

In search of visibility: an overview

REFLECTIONS ON THE GLASS CEILING would have remained a dream for me without recourse to the documents, records and notes I kept over the years, particularly during my twenty-five years with the Social Services Department of East Sussex County Council in England.

As a Black man, I have always found myself in unique places and situations that often required or necessitated personal sacrifices as well as professional, cultural and social adjustments. In part, and on reflection, these adjustments have shaped my life and experiences and made me the person I am today.

As I got older and progressed in my professional career, the urge to translate my dreams and experiences into a book grew. The catalyst and final motivation presented itself in late 1999 following my appointment as Service Manager for the countywide Substance Misuse and HIV/AIDS team.

I had been Acting Service Manager for almost a year and the feeling of achievement that the confirmation brought cannot be described in words. This was the pinnacle of my career and it symbolised so many things, at so many levels, including issues with my race and the 'glass ceiling' that had arguably prevented me from being promoted before. My appointment symbolised to me, and to others, that the glass ceiling could be cracked.

It was at this junction in my career that I began to reflect on what it meant to be the first Black service manager in a predominantly white local authority, particularly in East Sussex which, unlike cities like London or Birmingham, was not culturally diverse. Previous to this, I had held the record as the first Black social worker and the first Black senior practitioner. Other Black workers were present and existed in the organisation, but not at my professional level. While I was always proud of my achievements, I was aware that from the moment of that appointment – and, indeed, the higher up the hierarchy I progressed, both my race and my professionalism as a Black person would constantly be under scrutiny, and that I would also be seen as a role model and a mentor to other Black social workers. The latter prospect filled me with pride.

Throughout my twenty-six years with the local authority social services department and, as someone not brought up as a Black child in the local authority care system, I was frequently asked by my colleagues – and, occasionally, by service users – 'What is it like for you?' Born in Liberia,

West Africa, I spent my formative years in England and I had learned not to take seriously nor to always believe that the people asking such questions really wanted to hear the truth.

Reflecting on the question years later, I came to the conclusion that there was a lot more to it and that it required more than a one-word response of 'good' or 'bad' from me. To understand the relevance and curiosity behind the question, one needed to look at the Black and minority ethnic population of the county in which I worked at that time and how that was reflected in the workforce of the organisation. It did not take long to become aware and to conclude that the issue of race, more specifically being back, was implicit in their curiosity and questions.

Conducting my own research and enquiries, I became aware that prior to my employment with East Sussex, there had been few qualified Black social workers within the organisation and the local authority's experience and contact with Black people had been predominantly with those who were service users or domestic assistants in residential homes. The social work profession in the 1970s in that region was still regarded as a white middle-class profession.

The question of what it was like for me was also a difficult one to answer, but being asked that question repeatedly led me to reflect on my experiences over the years. Initially, I began to do so by making mental notes of those experiences which I felt were significant and then asking myself the same question. In many ways, this book is the consequence of that.

Although autobiographical, *Reflections on the Glass Ceiling* is also a narrative and my overdue response to the question of what it was like for me working as a social worker in a local authority in East Sussex during the 1980s and 1990s. It is about how I survived that experience for almost three decades.

The use of the term 'glass ceiling' is a considered one. The phrase is derived from the glass ceiling theory which came into prominence in the United States in the 1980s to describe the institutional barriers women faced in ascending career ladders, regardless of their qualifications or achievements. In later years, the phrase was broadened to include other categories, to describe situations where the advancement of a qualified person within the hierarchy of an organisation stops at a lower level because of some form of discrimination on the basis of race, gender, sexuality or disability. This discrimination may not be immediately apparent – hence the 'glass' – and it can also be the result of an unconscious bias or an unwritten or unofficial policy.

During my years with the local authority, my colleagues often commented to me that I was hitting or cracking the organisational glass ceiling because of sheer determination. Perhaps they saw my progress as a meteoric rise. I began as an assistant group worker and progressed to group leader, senior practitioner, service manager and practice manager. While there might have been an element of truth in my colleagues' analysis, I often wondered whether my career would have advanced further or more rapidly if I had not been a Black man.

After I finally decided to translate and put my reflections into writing, my next challenge was to identify my audience and who I intended to reach or target with my experiences and reflections. This has proved more difficult than I could possibly have imagined. In short, I want my story and career journey to inspire and motivate others.

During my career and years in social work, I was heavily involved with social work training and education, working with universities in the region. Social work training and education became my passion which stemmed from my two-year secondment in 2003 to Sussex University as a part-time tutor for social work and social care. I also remained active as a freelance trainer and practice educator years following my retirement from the local authority.

Reflections on the Glass Ceiling would not have been possible without the support of my wife, Karen, and children, Michael and Michelle. It would have also been impossible had I not kept essential and personal records and communications during my lengthy social work career. These records were very useful in my reflections on my experiences found in the pages that follow.

James Johnson
East Sussex, 2021

PART 1

Journey:
From Liberia To The West

CHAPTER 1

Early life in Liberia

I WAS BORN IN BUCHANAN, LIBERIA, WEST AFRICA, into what was regarded as a very middle-class, educated and politically active family. Liberia is Africa's oldest republic, founded and established in 1847 by freed American slaves. I was born in July 1947, the centenary, to the month and year, of Liberia's independence. My older brother, Charles, was two years old at the time.

Liberia is a unique African country with an equally unique history. It is situated on the West African coast, bordered by Guinea to the north, the Ivory Coast to the east and Sierra Leone to the north-west; the Atlantic Ocean lies to the south. It was established in 1847 by freed black American slaves. The Thirteenth Amendment, which formally abolished slavery in the United States, states: 'Neither slavery nor Involuntary servitude, except as a punishment for crime whereof the party shall have been duly convicted, shall exist within the United States or any place subject to their jurisdiction'. Thus white America and its politicians had to wrestle with the question of what to do with its newly freed slaves and their role in American society.

For many Americans, the idea that a Black person could be the equal of a white person was problematic. One idea posed was their resettlement in Africa. The Quaker movement in America took a lead role in advocating and facilitating the resettlement of freed Black slaves to Africa this and the American Colonisation Society (ACS), founded in 1817, was the result.

The ACS was a white philanthropic group seeking to remove Black people from America while spreading Christian influence abroad. It was supported by prominent American politicians like Abraham Lincoln and James Monroe. The US Congress also granted money to the ACS to support their purpose and, in 1822, the Society began transporting freed Black American slaves to West Africa, beginning with 86 men, women and children who left New York in 1820 on the *Mayflower of Liberia*. At the time, some regions in West Africa were given names based on their products and resources: the Grain Coast, formerly the Pepper Coast, because of its vegetation; the Gold Coast (Ghana) because of gold and the Ivory Coast because of its ivory. By 1822, the ship had brought a total of 15,000 former slaves and other Americans of African descent rescued from illegal slavery to the Grain Coast of West Africa, with the mission of establishing their own colony there in 1822.

The Grain Coast was already inhabited by indigenous Africans who had lived there from about the twelfth century. What was significant was that the new arrivals formed less than ten per cent of the population of the Grain Coast and maintained a different identity and lifestyle from the indigenous peoples. This was as a result of several factors. During their period of enslavement in America, most had acquired some degree of literacy and were able to communicate with those facilitating their resettlement; they also retained the American names given to them by their previous slave owners, such as Johnson, Tubman and Smith. Within a short period of time, they also began to impose their Western values on the majority indigenous population.

Many of the new arrivals were of mixed race, the result not of marriage but of sexual violence against Black women by their captors and owners. Although my ancestral history and heritage was not mixed race, my maternal grandmother often told us stories that her grandparents, in turn, had told her about life on southern plantations in America. My ancestral history and roots, including my surname, can be traced back to those first freed American settlers.

Referred to as Americo-Liberians following independence, they did not integrate with the indigenous people. The domination of the Americo-Liberians over the indigenous people would eventually lead to civil unrest, culminating in the military coup in 1980. On 26 July 1847, however, the new settlers issued a Declaration of Independence and formed a government with a constitution and a flag modelled after that of the United States, although with 11 stripes for each of the men who had signed the Constitution. The Grain Coast changed its name to Liberia, derived from the Latin word 'liber', meaning 'free' and became known as the home of freed American slaves. Refraining from taking on African identity, the settlers spoke English and established themselves quickly as the ruling class, despite being the minority group in the country. They had been educated within the American culture and married within their community. There was also a clear divide between where the indigenous peoples lived and where the Americo-Liberians lived. The latter settled on the south coast on the Atlantic Ocean, while the former lived further inland in an area commonly referred to at the time as 'the hinterland'. Most of the towns and cities in the south were given names that had connections to the United States. Monrovia, the capital, was named after James Monroe, the fifth US President, and Buchanan, my birthplace, was named after Liberia's first governor, Thomas, a cousin of James Buchanan, the fifteenth US President.

The major export industry in the country when I was growing up was rubber. The American industrialist and businessman Harvey S. Firestone Jr sought cheap land in Liberia to expand his empire. In 1926, The Firestone National Rubber Company, a US operation, began to operate the largest rubber plantation in the world in Harbel, a town some two miles from Roberts International Airport, the country's largest airstrip. The Firestone brand is today synonymous with tyres, and most of the rubber used to make tyres come from Liberia. Most wealthy Liberians began owning farms and investing in rubber. My grandfather and father had rubber farms, which were seen as a symbol of class and wealth. In addition to rubber, Liberia is also known internationally for having a flag of convenience; it is the second largest maritime registry in the world.

Charles and I had a happy childhood. We grew up in Buchanan, Grand Bassa County, about sixty miles from the capital, Monrovia, and in a culture that made us aware of the different social classes: those who were not Americo-Liberians were referred to as 'country people', mainly because they lacked education, spoke in over sixteen different local dialects and had African names. The dialect spoken in my county is called 'Bassa'. Although I can speak Bassa, I am no longer fluent and was never taught to write in the dialect. The Americo-Liberians also built and lived in colonial houses very similar to plantation houses in America.

Growing up in Liberia, the injustice surrounding us did not affect our way of life. We were aware at an early age of our privileged background and of our family's status within the community. We were well-positioned in society; our grandfather was the Chief Justice of the Supreme Court of Liberia. As a young child, I vividly remember President Tubman, Liberia's eighteenth president, visiting our home to meet us. We lived with our maternal grandparents in a family environment where two things were of paramount importance: religion and academic achievement. Living with our grandparents allowed our parents to travel to Monrovia to pursue their education at the University of Liberia. Consistent with the existing norms, this meant law for my father and domestic science, or 'home arts', for my mother.

As children, we had many close friends from similar backgrounds and, as young children and teenagers, our primary source of entertainment centred on playing soccer. Our only family activity on Sunday was going to church, in our case the Episcopal Church. We went in the morning and to Sunday School in the afternoon. After that, most families would go for a stroll on the beach to admire the Atlantic Ocean.

Our elementary education was obtained at a missionary school in Buchanan. I must have been less than ten years old when my brother and I, together with our older first cousin, Daniel, were sent to an expensive Catholic boarding school run mostly by Irish priests. The school was co-educational, but the boarders were male. Our parents were alumni of the same school, although my father had never boarded. It was very strict and rigid on discipline. Unlike most of the boarders though, Charles and I never converted to Catholicism, choosing to remain Episcopalian.

James Baldwin, the Black American writer and one of my favourite authors, once said, 'Children have never been very good at listening to their elders but they have never failed to imitate them.' When I reflect on my early life and education, Father Patrick was my favourite teacher and the role model I sought most to imitate. In retrospect, he had broken several glass ceilings: he was the first Black Liberian Catholic priest and went on to become the first Monsignor. More significantly, he was the first indigenous or 'native' Liberian to become a Catholic priest. At that time, the late 1950s, advanced education through religion was the only pathway available to indigenous people.

Father Patrick had a great influence on most of the young people at the school through his teaching, general advice and analysis of the political situation in the country. Outside my immediate family circle, father Patrick give me the foundation, the confidence and the tool for navigating my life and career pathway. I recall the many times he would endeavour to point out to us the corruptions and nepotism of the ruling Americo-Liberian class who controlled the economy of the country and denied access to jobs and education to the indigenous people. Father Patrick's message was that it was incumbent upon us, Liberia's future generation, to make a change. He really inspired us to learn and to have an awareness of the injustices in the country. Although, as young students, we may have thought he was too tough on us, his message has stayed with me. The only other Individual in recent years who has had the same impact on me was the first Black and former American president, Barack Obama, with his 'yes we can' message to African American.

Liberia's Constitution and flag were not the only things modelled after America; the education system was too. Like children on the other side of the Atlantic, after successfully completing my elementary education at the beginning of January 1963, aged 16, I enrolled in the ninth grade at Bassa High school for the January semester with the awareness that it would only be for six months. It was standard practice with West African parents, particularly those who were affluent, to select the careers or the career pathways for their children. In the majority of cases, the choice for boys was either medicine or law, while for girls it was in the domestic sciences. In my case, irrespective of any career ambitions I may have harboured, it had been instilled in me from an early age that I would become a doctor, the first in the family, while Charles, as the eldest, would naturally follow the path of our father and grandfather by going into the legal profession. My father boasted about having a future doctor in the family and went so far as to state that the family would have its own private medical clinic with 'Johnson's', the family surname, inscribed above its entrance.

In the 1950s and 1960s, another common practice prevalent among affluent West African parents was to send their children, boys and girls, abroad to be educated. Liberian families were no exception, though the one difference which stood Liberians apart from their West African neighbours was the choice of country, the latter usually choosing the United Kingdom, Belgium or France, in line with the historic colonial ties to their 'mother' nations. In the vast majority of cases, the parents themselves had followed the very same path.

Liberia was unique, however, because of its historic ties to the United States and its creation as a nation for freed slaves. Despite this, affluent Liberian parents commonly sent their children to England because the education system was perceived as superior to that of the States, and British good manners the best foundation in life for their children. In this, my parents were no different.

Years later, I came to the conclusion that the ostensible and perhaps unwritten reasons for Liberian parents sending their children abroad were probably twofold: yes, the children would benefit from having what their parents perceived to be 'good manners and a sound British education', yet there was also a more subtle reason. Having acquired a Western training and education, the children, upon reaching adulthood and with qualifications from prestigious colleges and universities, would return to their native countries with an advantage over their indigenous, less fortunate peers and consequently have better job prospects and political careers.

Growing up in Africa at the time, my only knowledge of England was either from the movies or from listening to the BBC World Service, with the chimes of Big Ben. Like most young Africans I had conjured up the most incredible images of London, its traditions, the Royal Family and their various palaces. Queen Elizabeth had made a day visit to Liberia during her tour of British colonies in West Africa in the early 1960s, but that was where my knowledge ended. Yet England was where I was going to be educated.

There were no medical schools in Liberia in the early 1960s, so it came as no particular surprise that in September 1963, aged just sixteen, I was sent away from the family and friends and everything I had known to a boarding school, not in London but in Hastings, a small town known for a historically important battle that hadn't even taken place there, situated on the south-east coast of England. All the arrangements with the school, Hastings Tutors, had been facilitated on my parents' behalf by family friends, in particular the student advisor at the Liberian Embassy in London.

Years later, as a psychology student, I was to reflect on those days and the impact of being separated from my family and of being sent to a foreign country and immersed in a different culture at so young an age. As a social worker, I would further reflect on separation and attachment theories and the work of John Bowlby, the British psychiatrist and psychoanalyst, and his interest in child development, as well as his pioneering work in attachment theory. I wondered at the time whether Bowlby's concepts were only limited and specific to children in the Western culture as supposed to my African culture. Bowlby's attachment theory seemed to imply that the damage to children which often results from the isolation and separation from their families.

The separation and isolation which I encountered as a child did have a negative impact on me during my adolescent years. I doubt if Bowlby's attachment theory resonated with African parents, and if it did, it seemed to take second place to their children acquiring a British education and British manners.

With a present population of five million, Liberia is still recovering from three major tragedies, two of them wars – the civil wars of 1989–90 and 1999–2001. The total death toll from both wars was estimated to have exceeded a quarter of a million people. The ebola epidemic in 2014–15 further resulted in the loss of 11,000 lives. Sadly again, Liberia, like many countries around the world, has been affected by the Covid-19 pandemic and, unlike countries like Britain and the United States, it lacks the health infrastructure for dealing with this new pandemic.

CHAPTER 2

Journey to England

AS THE AIRCRAFT BEGAN TO DESCEND INTO HEATHROW AIRPORT early that September morning in 1963, I was taken aback by the spectacular night lights of the City of London and its surroundings. At the airport, I was met by a family friend, the student advisor at the Liberian Embassy, who took me to the Embassy in London, where a hired taxi had been arranged to take me to Hastings in East Sussex, some 135 km away. The driver was wearing a coat and tie, which surprised me. Generally, in Africa, taxi drivers are poor, with limited education and they are unlikely to be able to afford a tie, let alone wear one to work.

Having left Liberia in mid-September at the start of the rainy season, I arrived in London on a damp and cold morning.

I remember being thrilled at the sight of the London red double-decker buses, having only seen them in the movies or on postcards. I was also somewhat surprised at how small the cars were and confused that they were driving on the left side of the road rather than on the right, like at home. Having heard so many stories in Liberia about London, I had built up an image of what to expect when I arrived. Rather disappointingly, the streets were not paved with gold, as some West African children at the time believed.

The journey to Hastings was an interesting experience. The driver tried to engage me in conversation and to point out some of the landmarks in London and the countryside; unfortunately, I could not understand his accent and it was obvious to me that he also had difficulties understanding my Liberian one. I had just left the security of my family and was experiencing my first hours in a totally different culture and climate and I was trying to make sense of my journey, while also trying to concentrate on the very different scenery. I was also conscious of the fact that I was travelling in a taxi with a stranger who was taking me to a place I didn't know and to a family I had never met nor spoken with.

It was a standard arrangement with the boarding school for foreign students to arrive a week prior to the beginning of the school term in order to begin to acclimatise to the weather. The school had arranged for me to be accommodated for a week with the Jones family. This was my first cultural experience: being looked after by a British family with a different racial and cultural background from mine. The

Jones family were very warm and friendly. They were also very proud of their Scottish heritage, although it was initially difficult for me to understand their accent.

The family consisted of a husband and wife, their adult son and their adopted daughter. There was also another daughter who lived and worked in another town. Mr and Mrs Jones also accommodated other students from Hastings Tutors, and when I arrived at their home that afternoon, I met two other students: Paul, another Liberian, who had been in England for a few years, and Jonathan, a student from Canada.

My baptism into British culture occurred at dinner time, just hours after arriving at my host family's home. Coming from a culture where rice was the staple food and where I had been accustomed to only eating food which had been cooked, it came as a culinary awakening to be presented with a vegetable salad as my first meal. Later, I came to understand that such salads were normal food in the summer months when the weather was good. This salad consisted of lettuce, tomatoes, beetroot and cucumber. The ingredients were familiar but unlike what I was used to in Liberia, where they were cooked. In my struggles to determine the order in which they had to be eaten, I was aware of being observed not only by my host family but also by the two other students, who, having lived in England for some years by then, had clearly adapted to the food. I remember as I sat at the table contemplating whether or not I could eat the food, I realised that the alternative meant not eating and ultimately starvation. So I decided to give it a go.

What that first experience taught me was an awareness of cultural differences in food and the simple things that most of us take for granted. The family had naturally assumed that I would be happy eating salad and therefore never bothered to ascertain my views. Because of my shyness and innate African politeness, I had to endure the agony and discomfort of chewing food which I found difficult to swallow. As a direct result of that experience, salad has never been a favourite dish of mine – and I certainly never wrote home about it.

What I distinctly remember about that evening, sitting at the dining table, was looking through the kitchen window into the family back garden and, to my delight, seeing a large apple tree with beautiful red apples. The apples looked similar to the imported ones we bought in Liberia. It was like manna from heaven, but unfortunately, the apples were never picked or eaten during my week stay with that family. It reminded me of the biblical forbidden fruit.

Following these early alien experiences, I thought things could not get more uncomfortable. I was wrong.

A few days later, with the weather still sunny, the family decided to have a picnic in Hastings Country Park, some three miles away from their home. The excitement that sunny Sunday afternoon was that we would all walk to the park, eat a picnic lunch and then walk back home. The menu consisted of cucumber sandwiches, which everyone except me seemed to relish. Many years later, I came to understand the social importance of the cucumber sandwich, that it is considered quintessentially English. However, at the time, it was another discomfiting experience, one that exacerbated my feeling of alienation. Many years later, as a group leader in a social work team which dealt with the recruitment and training of foster carers for hard-to-place teenagers and Black children, I was able to tap into my earlier experiences to create an awareness of cultural diversity in food and its importance. I believe I brought a richness to the understanding of these differences and how we service providers responded to them.

Another early cultural shock occurred that same week when I saw a young couple kissing in a public place. This public display of affection was completely alien to me as an African, living in a strict Christian country and from a family where that kind of demonstration of behaviour was done in private. It was all so alien.

Hastings Tutors was a relatively small and expensive private boarding school. The cost of boarding meant that all the foreign students came from wealthy families. The proprietor was a retired naval commander, Mr Smith, and his wife. There were no distinctive features about the school, which consisted of several large terrace houses near the local train station. Boarders at the school were male and overwhelmingly from overseas, particularly from West Africa, Ghana, Nigeria and the Middle East. There were also a number of local British day pupils. I liked the multicultural and racial make-up of the school. Like me, all the African students had been sent by their parents to achieve the same aim and objective: a sound British education.

I arrived by taxi from the Jones' home on a Sunday afternoon, the day before school started. Life at the Hastings Tutors was unexceptional, although I was shocked that first Monday morning to discover that one of our teachers was the son of Mr and Mrs Jones. No mention had been made of that fact. In terms of education, the focus was not so much on education but more on being trained to pass exams, the General Certificates of Education or O' levels. The six subjects chosen for me by the Commander as a prerequisite to pursuing my medical career were biology, chemistry, physics, English language, English literature and Latin.

Judging by the number of foreign students at Hastings Tutors, the school must have been held in high esteem by the African and Asian embassies in London, which were responsible mainly for the placements. This had more to do with training us to pass 'O' level exams than receiving a rounded education. The dress code was formal and we were required to wear tie and jacket daily except for sports. Like most boarding schools at the time, it had a head boy system and I became one in my final year. It was also strict in terms of behaviour; for instance, students were not allowed to run up or down stairs. Yet it was liberal in other ways: although the Commander and his wife were Catholics, students were encouraged to attend the church of their choice. I attended the local Church of England, Blacklands, in Hastings, which was similar to my Episcopal Church in Liberia. It was the church in which I was confirmed and, being the only Black person in the congregation, I got to know the pastor and his family well.

Although it was a boarding school, we did have the freedom to go into town in our spare time. Hastings was less than a mile away from the school and not far from the local railway station. This was an eye-opener. Apart from my vague knowledge of the British Empire, colonialism and the Windrush movement, when immigrants from Jamaica arrived in the United Kingdom from the late 1940s, they were met only with hostility and racism from what they had regarded as 'mother country'. I had grown up to believe that racism was an American issue which did not happen elsewhere. That perception changed within a few months of my arrival. After that first week with my host family, the Jones, my family and I assumed that this would be the permanent holiday arrangement for me. Sadly, when the Christmas holiday arrived the other Liberian student and I were sent to another host family, actually next-door neighbours to the Scottish family, while the Canadian student returned to the Jones.

Weeks after we had returned to school, I asked the Commander's wife why Calvin and I had been placed with a different host family, Mr and Mrs Kohler, while Jonathan, the Canadian student, had remained with the Jones. Her response to me has remained imprinted in my memory. She said that Jonathan's parents had said that they did not want him to spend Christmas with 'coloured' people. For me, the issue was not only what she said, but also the insensitivity of how it was said. I never raised the issue with my Canadian friend but wondered whether he was aware. Having spent my childhood and early adolescent years growing up in a Black affluent Liberian world where the only form of discrimination was based on class and ethnicity: Americo-Liberians and indigenous Liberians, rather than race, this was a personal, enlightening but unpleasant experience. Previously racial discrimination was an issue I had always associated with America and the civil rights movement at the time.

Reflecting on the issue years later, I wondered whether the headmaster's wife should have actually divulged that information to me. For the first time in my life, I became aware of racial differences and how they could affect me – that two Black students, little more than boys, were made to change host family purely to satisfy a white student's family. Surely Jonathan's parents were aware of the multiracial composition of Hastings Tutors, with boarders predominantly from West Africa and the Middle East? Yet it seemed that separating him from us at Christmas was important to them. This was a surprise to me because there was no evidence of racism within the school or between the students. The issue was never discussed with Calvin or Jonathan and, as teenagers, we carried on as friends. I am not even sure I shared this news with my family. My education was more important news.

This incident precipitated a number of questions in me; questions for which there were no simple answers or explanations at the time. My chosen career pathway then was medicine, but social issues such as these probably laid the foundation to my later training in psychology and social work, and my preoccupation with the latter as a tool for changing societal attitudes.

The Kohlers, an elderly couple, would remain my permanent host family for the duration of my education at Hastings Tutors. They were also Calvin's. It became obvious quickly that they were not wealthy and their detached home, although next door to the Jones', lacked many essential items, including a fridge, telephone and washing machine, items which I had taken for granted at home back in Liberia. Years later, I was surprised to learn that the couple were not married, given they were hosts for a wealthy private school. Apparently, 'Mrs Kohler' moved in with Mr Kohler initially as his carer, after he sustained a severe head injury during the war. My holidays with them were enjoyable, but still, it seemed an unusual set-up for hosts at that time.

One of the things I quickly had to come to terms with when I moved to England was the British love for animals, particularly dogs. My first host family had two dogs and the second one had a large sheepdog which they treated as an extension of the family. I remember being aghast when, following Sunday dinners, the landlady scooped some of the leftovers onto one of the plates from which we had just eaten dinner and placed it on the floor for the dog. This after-dinner ritual occurred each evening. When the conversation arose one evening about animals in Liberia, I had to be honest and tell them that while we did have dogs and cats at home, the main difference was that they were never allowed in the house, particularly dogs.

After three years at Hastings Tutors, I obtained the required number of GCEs and was ready to move on to higher education. My next move would take me to Hastings College of Further Education to pursue 'A' Levels in Chemistry, Physics and Zoology in preparation for my medical training.

As the Kohlers were not able to provide full-time accommodation for me, the Commander's wife recommended another family, Mr and Mrs Evans, who, in many ways, I came to regard as my family away from home. Their terraced home was basic and lacked many essential facilities as well. However, on reflection, family homes in England generally, in the 1960s, lacked many of the facilities I was used to in Liberia, and these families often provided accommodation to students because they depended on the extra income. However, to both me and my family in Liberia, my education was far more important than my physical environment.

When I went to live with them, the Evans had two daughters, but had not long lost their eldest son in a train accident. Sadly Mr Evans, who was a heavy smoker, also appeared to suffer from ill health. One summer morning, when I was about to travel to Heathrow for my summer holiday in Liberia, he was taken to hospital by ambulance. He died of lung cancer a few days later. I regret not having been able to fly back to attend his funeral. It was obviously a difficult time for the family. Later, I was glad to help by being supportive and getting the family to talk to me and share their memories of the husband and father they had lost.

My landlady found inspiration in religion, however, and

was a regular Sunday evening churchgoer. After her husband's death, I began walking with her to church most Sundays. When their older daughter, a hairdresser, moved to London though, the rest of the family followed. Despite this, I maintained close contact with the family even when I lived in America and Liberia. When my family and I returned to England, we were delighted that Mrs Evans was able to visit us in Hastings and meet my wife and children. She died a few years ago in Bromley, Kent. My presence at the funeral was acknowledged by the vicar during his sermon, which pleased me. It was like a family reunion and a pleasure to meet family members I hadn't seen for over ten years.

My move to Hastings College of Further Education in 1977 was a new and liberating social experience, and a far cry from life at Hastings Tutors. The college population was more multicultural, with students from all over the world, particularly Asia and Africa. There were also five other Liberian students studying at the college. Providing accommodation to foreign students was good business for private landlords and host families.

Socially, nothing could have been more exciting and thrilling than being a teenager in England in the 1960s. Unlike America, where the struggle for civil rights defined that decade, the period is remembered in England for its music and fashion, and the social life at the college reflected this. For me, college life meant studying all week and going to social or dance clubs at weekends.

Outside college many of us hung out at dance clubs. There

were several such clubs locally but the Witch Doctor, on the seafront in nearby St Leonards-on-Sea, was by far the most popular and most frequented because of its atmosphere and music, which was soul and Motown. It was the place to be at the time to meet other young people, a place where racial barriers did not seem to exist. A peculiarity I never understood at these clubs was that the white British lads would spend the evening at the club around the bar area, usually holding a glass of beer, while the white ladies would place their handbags on the floor and dance with each other around their bags.

One particular night, I was at the club with a Liberian friend when we noticed two white teenagers dancing together. We plucked up the courage and approached them to dance. The young lady whom I danced with told me her name was Karen. Chatting to her, I discovered that she was also a student at Hastings College, although I had never seen her. This was not that surprising: as a pre-medical student I had my own group and, as a business student, she had hers. The two groups always sat separately in the college canteen.

Karen and I became friends after that night and began to meet regularly at college and to go to the Witch Doctor on Saturday nights. The friendship turned into more; our relationship soon became serious and I was invited to meet her family.

As I approached the final year of my studies, I began to seriously consider moving to America to begin my medical training. At that time, most Liberians studying in England went on to matriculate in the United States. At the end of my two years at Hastings College, I returned briefly to Liberia to make preparations to study in the States. It was sad having to leave England, not to mention Karen, and Hastings, the town where I had happily spent some of my teenage years. However, it was a move in the direction that was planned and I left always believing that I would return to England. Karen and I, of course, remained in touch.

I had travelled home for summer holidays several times during my schooling abroad, but this occasion was different. I spent my first Christmas in seven years with my family at home in Liberia. Emotionally it was a good experience being able to reconnect with my culture and identity. One of the first things I tried to do, albeit with limited success, was to undo my formal Britishness and to lose my English accent and foreign ways of behaving. I felt that I needed to reintegrate myself into my 'native' culture and way of life, even though I was aware that my time at home would be consumed with making plans for matriculating to the United States. Unlike the plans that were made by my parents for me to go to England when I was a young teenager, as an adult I was now steering my future and the decision to go to America, even though I remained financially dependent on them.

Years later, I went through a period of reflection over the psychological consequences and damage to children who are separated from their parents for a perceived better life abroad. I like to think I was not severely affected by that, although there were times when I felt the need to be with my family and not with people I knew for only limited periods of time. Looking back now, as both a father and grandfather, I can say without any doubt at all that there would never have been any circumstances that would have precipitated us sending our children to boarding school, let alone one in a foreign country. Following the military coup in Liberia in April 1980, I became separated from my family for several months and I saw the effect that separation had on my son, who was only four years old at the time.

Looking back at my late teenage years, I wonder how other African teenagers who were also sent abroad like me coped with their surroundings and adjusted to being in a place which they could not call home. Looking back, my experiences were similar to those of the Windrush generation, who believed they were coming to England, their mother country, only to be met with discrimination. The question 'who am I?' was one with which I struggled. It is perhaps no surprise that while studying psychology and in my career in social work, I started to reflect on issues such as separation and loss and the impact they had on my own social and emotional development.

The time at home was bitter–sweet. It was temporary as I was about to embark on the next phase of my education and I was trying to gear myself up to the next separation from my friends and family, this time of my own making, in America.

When I was growing up in Liberia, our only source of news and information came from two radio stations in the country. One was state owned and the other was a religious station owned by missionaries. It was commonly referred to as radio ELWA, Eternal Love Winning Africa. In our household, which was religious, we only listened to ELWA on Sunday and I recall most of the religious programmes and music as being broadcast from Grand Rapids, Michigan, in the United States. Practically everyone in Liberia had heard of Grand Rapids via ELWA, so when I began my research for colleges or universities in the United States, Grand Rapids and the state of Michigan were at the top of my list. Eventually the list was narrowed down to Olivet College, a co-educational private liberal arts college in Michigan. I forwarded my application and, within six weeks, I received a letter of acceptance for the January term.

CHAPTER 3

Experiencing the
American Dream

I ARRIVED IN AMERICA IN EARLY JANUARY 1970, IN
THE MIDDLE OF WINTER, which in Michigan provided an
uncomfortable freezing contrast with the weather in Africa.
I arrived two weeks early in order to spend some time with
a Liberian friend, Clarence, who was studying at Aquinas
College, a small Roman Catholic liberal arts college in Grand
Rapids, before I travelled on to Olivet.

The weather was severe, temperatures below freezing,
snow literally covering the entire landscape. I had never
encountered such severe cold weather, not even during my
winters in England – which I had just experienced again
briefly when I stopped off to see Karen on my way to the

States. Despite the inclemency of the climate, I fell in love with Grand Rapids within a few days of my arrival. Michigan is a beautiful state, known for the Great Lakes, and while the weather could be extreme, in addition to its severe winters, it also had hot summers when tornadoes were very common.

Almost every Liberian of my generation would have heard of Grand Rapids, Michigan, through the ELWA, Eternal Love Winning Africa broadcasting station. Established in 1951 by missionaries, most of the programmes and preaching on ELWA came from Grand Rapids, Michigan. In my household growing up, ELWA was the only station we listened to on Sundays.

Because of ELWA, I had a picture in my mind of Grand Rapids when I arrived in early January for the second semester at Olivet College. I got to meet some of Clarence's friends, who included Americans and also Africans from Nigeria and Sierra Leone. They told me that Olivet was a small town and did not have much to offer socially. They suggested that I look at some of the colleges in Grand Rapids. It did not take much to be persuaded.

My search for colleges in Grand Rapids finally narrowed down to Calvin College, another liberal arts college. The college was founded in 1876 and had strong ties to the Christian Reformed Church and Calvinism. During my research on Calvin, what impressed me most was that it was ranked number one among the regional colleges in the Midwest. I immediately telephoned the admissions office and explained who I was and what I wanted. Not long after, I was invited in for a meeting and interview, where I duly presented my

British qualifications as evidence of my academic achievement. The admissions office contacted me to inform me that I had been accepted and could start the next week.

I began my studies at Calvin during a particularly tumultuous and interesting time in America: one, like now, of racial tension and student unrest. The Thirteenth Amendment may have abolished slavery and led to the establishment of Liberia but, in practice, America still had, and has, a long way to go before achieving racial equality. President Lyndon B. Johnson had signed the Civil Rights Act six years earlier, on July 2, 1964, and that prohibited discrimination on the basis of race, colour, religion, sex and national origin in public. Tragically though, on April 4, 1968, Dr Martin Luther King, Jr, the civil rights leader who had fought so hard for the bill to be passed and for desegregation, was assassinated. America was, in addition, involved in the Vietnam War (1955–74), a conflict that divided public opinion and culminated in student unrest across the country.

In May 1970, a few months after my arrival in Michigan, the media reported the Kent State University shooting. In response to students demonstrating against the bombing of Cambodia, the Ohio National Guard was summoned. Sadly, their intervention resulted in four students being shot dead and a further nine being wounded. This tragic event led to the temporary closure of universities and college campuses across the country. For me, it was a shock. I hadn't experienced such violence before, and seeing these events first-hand made me apprehensive about living in America, but I overcame my fears by convincing myself that it was unlikely any harm would come to me. Plus, Clarence, the friend whom I had met up with, did not seem too bothered about the shooting events.

I commenced my studies at Calvin College, now Calvin University, in the second term of the American academic year. On campus, it was interesting to observe that the student population at Calvin, which was overwhelmingly white and predominantly of Dutch ancestry, did not appear to reflect the demographic profile of Grand Rapids. Although I was not aware of the number of people living in Grand Rapids at the time, one of the first things that stuck me was the high ratio of Black people. Having said that, I did not observe or experience any problems with race or racism, perhaps because Calvin College was different from other colleges in America. A liberal arts, religious, co-educational college, it followed the teaching of John Calvin, the French theologian and reformer. John Calvin was a major leader of the Protestant Reformation. Calvinism is based around the absolute power and supremacy of God and emphasises predestination.

As a freshman student, I enrolled on a pre-med course. In addition, I was required to include a number of elective subjects which, in my case, included psychology and sociology. At the time, psychology was very popular among university students who were seeking answers to the 'who am I?' question and trying to understand themselves. I became very interested in the subject because I was seeking the tools to explore and understand my experiences and make sense of my world. It worked and by the end of freshman year, I had more or less concluded that psychology was more appealing to me than medicine. At the start of my sophomore year, I decided to change direction towards a major in psychology and a minor in sociology.

As I had anticipated, my father did not favour this because he was determined for me to be a doctor. For the first time in my life, however, I felt in control, especially as I was no longer dependent on the bank of mum and dad. This was my decision. I was now funding my own college education and striving to be financially independent of my parents. As an African, it was a difficult dilemma, but one which my parents understood. I was doing what I wanted to do, albeit with difficulties, as I no longer wanted to rely on their financial support. To achieve this meant that I had to work

My student visa and immigration status permitted me to do paid work for a maximum of sixteen hours a week during college term. There were no restrictions to my working hours during the summer holidays. This was when I discovered that America was more than a melting pot of nations: it was also a land of immense opportunity. Part-time campus jobs were in abundance and many students took advantage of this to subsidise their income. During my registration at the start of the term, I was offered regular campus employment which ranged from cleaning toilets, working and shovelling snow off the campus pathways to working in the gym dispensing equipment to students. While shovelling snow, I met Phil, a final year biology major, and we decided to share a house, eventually renting a four-bed and subletting rooms to two other students from Calvin. The arrangement worked well.

I had another fortunate experience just prior to registration. All incoming freshman students were allocated a mentor to assist them with the process and give an introduction to the college. Mike, my mentor, was a white American senior law student whose family had well-established connections with the college and the Christian Reformed Church. Mike's father was Head of Education at Calvin and his mother was an alumnus. His younger sister, Karen and her fiancé, Tom, were also both sophomore students.

Mike took me under his wing and during one of our many conversations, I mentioned that I played football, or soccer as it is called in the States. He informed me that his sister's fiancé was the captain of the college soccer team and wasted no time in introducing me to his family and future brother-in-law. His parents soon became my 'American parents', in every sense of the term. They were regular churchgoers at Calvin Christian Reformed Church, a Protestant denomination faith with roots in the Dutch Reformed Church. The family often invited me to attend services with them. After some months, I began to attend regularly. I was always the only Black person in the congregation, and because of this it seemed everyone wanted to talk to me at the end of service. Grand Rapids seemed like a religious town with many churches and different denominations and faiths. The more I observed the activities and genuineness of the congregation at Calvin's church, the more inspired I became by the church and its doctrine and teaching. This eventually led to my conversion to Calvinism.

I also joined the soccer team. The college played in the Michigan Intercollegiate Athletic Association, MIAA. Playing in forward position on the college first team, I received numerous college and regional awards, including the MVP (Most Valuable Player) award in my senior year. I became accustomed to being the rare Black person on campus, a factor that resulted in me becoming well-known and my name appearing in the college weekly newspaper.

The generosity of the people at Calvin, including Mike's family, enabled me to fulfil a second dream, to facilitate Karen's travel to the States. She had been working in Hastings and planning to join me In Grand Rapids. In 1971, within a year of my arrival in Grand Rapids, Karen arrived on a student visa to attend Davenport, a business college in Grand Rapids. She stayed with Mike's parents until she became settled. Later, she worked as a nanny to an American family, Barbara and Ray, who had three children. The family lived In Jenison, Michigan, some fifteen miles outside Grand Rapids.

Through our respective colleges, Davenport and Calvin, and social networks, Karen and I got to meet many other African students studying at colleges in the area. The majority of the students were Nigerians who had fled the Biafran War, the civil conflict which had broken out in 1967.

Finally together again, Karen and I decided to embark on the next phase of our journey and, on August 21, 1971, we were married in the Sunshine Chapel in Grand Rapids. It was a small but memorable event with our newly established friends. The day before the wedding, we received a cable from her parents to say that her mother was travelling to the wedding. This was good news for us, especially as my family were not able to attend. My best man was Clarence and Karen's maid of honour was Mike's sister, Karen. Our honeymoon was spent on Lake Campbell in Michigan, where we had both been working.

There were many opportunities at the time for part-time and summer jobs that related to my field of study. During my first summer holiday, I worked as a college counsellor on Upward Bound, a residential educational programme at Calvin aimed at providing Black, Hispanic and inner-city high-school students with additional educational courses to prepare them for college. All the counsellors on the programme were university students and predominantly Black. Our primary role was to mentor the students and provide them with support and guidance. This was my first experience of mentoring, and I have continued to do it all my life, because it is something that connects me mentally and emotionally to the needs and understanding of others, particularly those from different ethnic backgrounds. As a mentor, I feel that I can make a difference, as well as being a positive role model to my mentees.

The early summers in the States gave me the opportunity to appreciate the beauty of Lake Campbell, particularly through my experience of Tall Turf. A summer camp for inner-city children, located some seventy miles from Grand Rapids, Tall Turf was located on 240 acres of wilderness. The children came to stay in cabins on the lake shore, supervised by camp counsellors, of which I was one. Over the summer, groups of campers arrived for a ten-day structured outdoor programme that included archery, swimming, nature walks and horse riding.

The camp was funded by the Christian Reformed Church to provide urban children with the experience of life in the country. I was a camp counsellor during the first summer and was then promoted to activities coordinator for the second. Karen also worked at the camp that second year as a kitchen assistant. Our honeymoon was actually spent on the camp, combining work with pleasure.

Those summer experiences gave me some insight into social class division and race issues in America and the impact of some, such as poverty and racism, on inner-city communities like Chicago and Detroit, where many of these children and young people lived. The counsellors at Upward Bounds and Tall Turf were predominantly Black college or university students. This seemed important in terms of mentoring and being positive role models to young Black city kids. I was conscious of the fact that although I was Black, I was not a Black American and this made me aware of differences even within the same looking racial group.

At the time, it seemed to be a common summer camp ritual to raise the American flag in the mornings while reciting the national anthem. At Tall Turf, we agreed to replace the national anthem with the singing of what had become known as the 'Black national anthem': 'Lift Every Voice and Sing', written by James Weldon Johnson in 1900. Johnson was a Black American statesman, author, lawyer, educator, composer and civil rights activist. He was prominent in the Harlem Renaissance of the 1920s and also headed the NAACP, the National Association for the Advancement of Coloured People. 'Lift every voice and sing' is a song of hope and inspiration.

My experiences as a counsellor prepared me for my next part-time job at Baxter, an inner-city community centre. The job involved working a couple of hours in the evening with young teenagers, mostly Black lads, who came to play basketball and pool. Baxter was funded by the local Christian reformed church for teenagers in the Grand Rapids area. Like my earlier experiences, the cultural atmosphere at the community centre reflected the racial divide in the town. I even had a personal experience of this. I recall an incident that happened at the centre. On this particular afternoon, I answered the office telephone when it rang. After a few seconds of the customary greetings, the caller, a Black woman, recognising that my accent was different, and asked me directly: 'Is you Black, or is you White'? I responded by telling her that I was Black. When I later reflected on the incident and why the woman needed to know my colour, I thought it probably had to do with my unfamiliar accent. Nevertheless, it got me thinking about myself, a Black African, being mistaken by a Black woman for a white man purely on that basis. The woman had assumed, based on my mixed British and Liberian accent, that I was not a Black American and therefore could not be trusted with the care of her son.

This incident triggered me to think about my own identity and how I would define myself and social group. I always identified myself as a Black African, but in itself that has so many different layers. Similar differences are being played out today in Britain in terms of how Black and ethnic minority groups want to be identified and categorised.

Of the various part-time jobs I held, the one which was particularly relevant to my future career and would later become my 'permanent' part-time employment was as a psychiatric aide at a Christian hospital. I worked in the adolescent unit where the programme was based on behaviourism and the theory of BF Skinner, one of the most influential of American psychologists at the time. Skinner developed the theory of operant conditioning: the idea that behaviour is determined by its consequences, be they reinforcements or punishments, which make it more or less likely that a behaviour will occur again. At the time this theory had a profound influence on me because it showed that with the right stimulus and incentives, negative behaviour can be modified or replaced.

My hard work and tenacity paid off in June 1974 when I graduated with a BA degree in psychology. Along with this though came the difficult decision of what to do next, and I felt I needed at least a year to make that decision. However, I was also aware that my immigration status only allowed me to work while I was in full-time education. My solution was to enrol at Western Michigan University to pursue a postgraduate course in behavioural psychology. Western Michigan was also regarded as the centre for behaviourism.

Based in Kalamazoo, the university also rather handily had a branch in Grand Rapids.

I attended for a year and gained some credits towards a masters' degree, as well as a greater understanding of behaviourism. However, after a year, Karen and I came to a joint decision regarding what we wanted to do next – go to Liberia.

I had spent over ten years of my life, much of it my formative years, living outside Africa, absorbing the cultures of Europe and America. It made me reflect on my identity and who I was. Life and education in America made me aware that identity gives one a sense of belonging. This period coincided with the famous song 'Say it loud, I'm Black and I'm proud' by the African American soul singer James Brown. However, in my case, and despite the greatness of America and the abundance of opportunities, I wanted to reconnect with my Liberian roots and culture and see what contributions I could make to my country.

By the early 1970s, the Liberian government under President William Tolbert had embarked on a 'Liberianisation' drive to attract qualified citizens living abroad back to the country and take up the jobs being given to expats. Although I wouldn't be coming back as the doctor my father had wanted, I felt I could contribute to my native country's development. We also wanted to start a family and Karen and I wanted our children to be born in my country of origin.

It wasn't an easy decision to make though. Michigan,

despite its long, frozen winters and overbearingly hot summers had become my home away from home. Karen and I had fallen in love with America and had made lifelong friends in Grand Rapids, as well as people we considered family. It had been five great years for me, four for Karen, yet we were both determined that Liberia would be our next destination.

CHAPTER 4

Back to Africa

OUR JOURNEY TO LIBERIA TOOK US VIA ENGLAND, where we spent a few months with Karen's parents in Hastings, catching up with old friends. In the end, I left for Liberia a few months ahead of Karen, who was now expecting our first child. We had decided to live in Monrovia, Liberia's capital. Fortunately for us, although my family lived in Buchanan, my father owned a four-bedroom bungalow in Monrovia, and it had recently been vacated by my younger sister, Clora, and her family. This was to be our base until we were financially secure and able to purchase a home for ourselves.

Returning to Liberia presented me with a number of cultural shocks. In the mid-1970s, when I left America and England to settle in Liberia, my wardrobe and appearance reflected the popular fashion for young Black men: platform shoes, flared trousers and a beard, topped off with a large Afro. I was disconcerted by the shock and embarrassment my appearance appeared to cause. Family and close friends told me in no uncertain terms that this 'Western' image in Liberia gave out the message that I wasn't serious. My mother warned me to 'tone down' my appearance, while others bluntly said that unless I changed my look I would never get a decent, respectable job in the country, even with my qualifications.

So, what was the expected Liberian attire and dress code at the time? It wasn't the typical African gown and attire worn in many West African countries, but rather the white 'swear-in suit', the nickname given to the open-neck style of French safari suits popularised in 1971 by William Tolbert, the new president. As the story goes, when President Tubman died suddenly in a London clinic, Vice-President Tolbert was on his farm in the interior of the country, miles outside of Monrovia. In keeping with the Constitution, the vice-president had to be sworn in as president within twenty-four hours. Serious attempts were made to bring Tolbert back to Monrovia, but the car bringing him back reportedly broke down; immediate efforts were made to acquire another vehicle for the long journey. When Tolbert finally arrived, it was in the safari suit which he had worn on his farm. He was wearing that very same suit when he was sworn in as president. The 'Swear-In Suit', as it became known, represented the new national dress code for businessmen and politicians, replacing the Americo-Liberian coat and tie which had been worn by

Tolbert's nineteen predecessors.

As the saying goes 'When in Rome, do as the Romans do'. I actually admired the suits, which were ideal for the hot climate, so heeding family advice, I immediately had three such suits made for myself, including a white one. I had a haircut, but refused to remove my goatee. The transformation seemingly paid off: after a few weeks of job searching and also using my family contacts and influence, I was offered a position as counselling and guidance administrator within the personnel department of the Liberian Electricity Corporation, or the LEC as it was popularly referred to in the country. Like most major corporations, the LEC was a government corporation.

The position had just been created on the recommendation of the World Bank as part of a loan agreement in order to address the problems that the corporation was experiencing with employees who were either not showing up for work due to alcohol misuse or were absent because of some other medical problem. My role was to provide guidance and counselling to those referred to the personnel department by their managers. The previous practice had been to dismiss employees without considering the underlying factors and causes for their absenteeism. Both employees and their managers welcomed my role and in a short time we were receiving reports of a reduction in both absenteeism and termination of employment. It was a busy job, but one which I really enjoyed.

Life in Liberia was beginning to look great and Karen finally arrived in time for our first Christmas in Africa. I had been in Liberia for three months. Added to our joy was the birth of our son Michael, four months later in April 1976. We had employed a full-time nanny prior to Michael's birth and after about a year, Karen started work as an administrator with the American Cooperative School in Monrovia.

After a few years with the LEC, there was a reorganisation and I was transferred to the commercial department as director of administration. This post, which lasted for over twelve months, made it possible for me to attend several management training courses and seminars at the Institute of Public Administration. With these new qualifications, I returned to the personnel department as director. Along with my promotion came many benefits and privileges, including a company car and driver. I was only in my early thirties and resisted having a driver – I was quite capable of driving myself. However, I came to realise that such a refusal would have meant that the man would lose his job, in a country with such a divide between the rich and poor, so I accepted the perk.

Our social life In Monrovia soon took a different dimension with a new network of friends and neighbours, most of whom had similarly just returned home to Liberia from America and Europe in response to the 'Liberianisation' policy and drive. A few of our friends also had foreign wives. Liberianisation was intended to redress the previous practice of giving jobs which Liberians were qualified for to foreign nationals from Europe and America. Another key feature of President Tolbert's Liberianisation drive was the building of low-cost houses on two estates in Monrovia, which were only available to Liberians to purchase or lease. The Matada estate had recently been built and was more upmarket and secluded than the first estate, Carbra. The Matada estate was where we purchased our first house: a four-bedroom, two-storey detached house with front and back gardens, located on the outskirts of Monrovia. It was an affluent community. A few of our Liberian friends, who had returned from America, had also purchased houses in the same estate. It was a great joy to be proud home owners for the first time.

After over a century of being seen as the beacon of independence and self-government in West Africa, the Liberia to which I returned was fundamentally unchanged from my memories of what it had been like when I had left in the early 1960s to go to school. Granted there was a new government in place, but the social issues and class divisions remained, although the latter had become more subtle, particularly the divide between the Americo-Liberians and the indigenous people. It was so easy to pretend, as I did many times, that everything was fine and that inequality and poverty did not exist.

What fascinated me was how the different groups and classes were able to live together in the same neighbourhood, albeit under different circumstances and in totally different lifestyles. Our immediate neighbours in Monrovia included a university professor and his family, a doctor, and a close relative of former Liberian president William Tubman. There was also a poor indigenous family who lived in a mud hut, without electricity and running water. I remember one Christmas when we were all celebrating at one of the neighbour's houses, we heard screaming and crying emanating from the mud hut. Upon enquiry, we were told that two babies in the household had just died from malaria. That incident and the issue of poverty for that family stayed in my memory for a considerable time. The following day, I woke up feeling ashamed that we had failed to interrupt our social activity to assist or support a family who had just lost their babies simply because they could not afford the cost of malaria medication. Reflecting on that event was probably one of the triggers to a embarking on a social work career in order to make a difference in helping others.

After living in Liberia for three years, we noticed that socially and politically things were starting to change, particularly in Monrovia. The president's absolute authority not only began to come under public scrutiny but was challenged. Growing social and political unrest and mass demonstrations against the government and the elite ruling class, which was deemed to be corrupt and nepotistic, became commonplace. Since independence, the country had been ruled by a one political party elite system led by Americo-Liberians. In 1975, the returned Liberian diaspora began to agitate for the development of a new party. The Progressive Alliance of Liberia, or PAL, was established in 1978. Led by Gabriel Baccus Matthews, it espoused a quasi-Marxist approach to Black nationalism and presented a major challenge to the True Whig Party government. With this development, one could sense tension and uncertainty in Monrovia. The tipping point came when in early April 1979, the government increased the cost of rice, the country's staple food, from $22 per 100-pound bag to $26.

In response to this move, PAL called for a peaceful demonstration in Monrovia. What was meant to be a nonviolent protest soon turned into something very different. The April 14 'Rice Riot' lasted for several days and resulted in the death of forty protesters, with hundreds more injured. There was widescale looting and destruction of properties in the city. A dusk-to-dawn curfew imposed by the government failed to curb the violence. The Rice Riot exposed the president's precarious hold on power and set the scene for what was to follow. PAL was banned as a political party and its leaders were imprisoned and charged with treason. Although some form of normality was restored in the capital, Karen and I sensed that this was the beginning of something much bigger and possibly more destructive for Liberia. In the months that followed, there was a gradual exodus from the country of the many Liberians who had returned home during the Liberianisation drive just years earlier.

On a happier note for us, during that period of uncertainty, was the birth of our daughter Michelle, on 5 April 1980, just under a year after the Rice Riot. We moved into Matada in April 1980, the week of Michelle's birth.

A week after Michelle's birth, one of my colleagues threw a birthday party and invited me and some of our colleagues from the corporation, including our managing director. As luck would have it, I decided to leave the party at about 10 p.m. and drive home because Karen and the children were at home alone. The journey back was my regular route which took me past the Executive Mansion in Monrovia. It seemed unusually quiet that night as I drove past.

In the early hours of 12 April, we were awakened by the sound of machine gun fire in the distance. Similarly loud noises were emanating from streets adjoining ours. Exactly a year before, there had been a rice riot in Monrovia and since then the political atmosphere in the Monrovia had become a daily conversation and a cause for concern. Karen and I woke up and quickly tuned into the Liberia Broadcasting Station. Within a few minutes we heard an announcement being made by the leader of a group which identified themselves as the People's Redemption Council, or PRC. The radio announcer proceeded to inform the country that the PRC had taken over the station and that President William Richard Tolbert Jr had been assassinated and the country was now under the leadership of Master Sergeant Samuel K. Doe.

Prior to that announcement, I had never heard of Samuel Doe of the PRC, which was apparently made up of semi-educated, enlisted army soldiers from the indigenous tribes. They stormed the Executive Mansion at midnight and brutally murdered the president, probably about the time I was driving home by way of the Executive Mansion. The first act of the Council was to declare a dusk-to-dawn curfew, accompanied by the strong message that anyone found breaking it would be shot.

Throughout the day, there were radio announcements from

the Council. One of the earliest gave a list of the names of prominent Liberian government officials who were instructed to 'turn themselves in'. Many of the names I recognised, including the name of my managing director who, it seemed, had already been arrested at the party I had left. The names were being broadcast with frightening and frequent regularity and it seemed that with each announcement a new name had been added to the list. I spent the rest of the morning glued to the radio, anticipating my own name.

Karen and I were shocked a few days after the coup when it was announced that the army had decided to occupy all the houses on the Matada estate where we lived. We were given just four hours to vacate our homes. It was a painful experience for me having to watch soldiers move into our home that evening. With soldiers on the streets with machine guns and road blocks it would have been unsafe to travel out of Monrovia to Buchanan. Fortunately, we had somewhere to go and we returned to my father's bungalow. It was then that I concluded that my Liberian dream was over. The military coup did more than shatter dreams and ambitions; it destroyed lives. It was a tribal coup and many citizens and cabinet ministers of the Americo-Liberian descent were subsequently executed by firing squad.

Members of the PRC began sending out letters to businesses and corporations demanding that they only employ certain groups of people. As director of personnel for the Liberia Electricity Corporation, this was the beginning of my nightmare with the PRC. Each day, I would receive written instructions to employ certain individuals, irrespective of their qualifications or suitability. As a way of addressing this, the senior management of the corporation decided to prepare a standard letter of response to the volume of requests we were receiving. It began with an acknowledgement of the request and recommendation. The letter then continued with a paragraph of regret that at the present time we had no vacancies; however, we would retain the recommendation on file should a suitable vacancy arise in the near future.

The personal test came when I received a letter from the deputy leader of the council requesting that I employ a particular person as my deputy director of personnel. Naïvely I replied using the approved letter the management team had approved. A few days later, while looking out of my office window onto the car park, I saw an army jeep entering the premises. I watched as three soldiers with machine guns jumped out of the jeep before it had even come to a halt. Nervously, I observed them heading toward the personnel department. They entered, ignored the reception staff and walked into my office. They demanded to know why I had refused to employ the candidate that the PRC had nominated as my deputy by the council. When I explained that I already had a deputy and that there was no other vacancy in my office, one of them asked me an interesting question. He wanted to know how I would have responded if the previous president and administration had written me a similar letter. What I felt like saying, but obviously could not, was that the previous president was an educated man who would not have written such a letter.

In most government offices in Liberia it had been customary to display a photograph of the president. Unfortunately, it had not occurred to me to remove the portrait of the deposed President Tolbert from my office wall. This was a red rag to a bull. My armed intruders questioned my motives while removing the photograph. I guess I took the coward's way out when I was being questioned by suggesting to the soldiers that perhaps they needed to talk to my boss, the new managing director of the corporation, a qualified engineer appointed by the PRC. I pointed them in the direction of his office and as they headed there, I left for the day. I could have easily been shot dead during that confrontation.

A few days after that encounter, we had a surprise guest at our senior management weekly meeting: Master Samuel K. Doe himself and his machine gun-clad entourage of soldiers. The purpose of his visit was to instruct our director of rural electrification to install electricity in a certain town with immediate effect. Seated next to our director, with both of us facing the Master Sergeant across the table, my colleague tried to say that the corporation had recently done a feasibility study on electrification in that area and that the inhabitants could not afford the cost. He was interrupted by Doe, who informed him that he did not know what feasibility meant but what he wanted was immediate electricity in that town. With that demand, he and his team departed. Those two experiences for me confirmed that my Liberian dream was definitely finished.

Prior to the military coup, most people in the Western world had limited knowledge of Liberia, other than its connection to freed American slaves. In West Africa, the image of Liberia was that of a stable, independent country. The coup shattered that image, along with the dreams and aspirations of many of its citizens.

The national seal of the country has inscribed at its top 'The love of liberty brought us here', a clear reference to the plight of the early Black settlers from America who established the republic in 1847. My love of liberty led Karen and me to appraise our options. Regrettably, after almost five years of living our Liberian dream, the events following the brutal and barbaric military coup meant that the safety of our family became our priority. From what we had seen and experienced in the few weeks of the PRC's rule, we did not believe that the country could recover economically and politically. It was time to leave Liberia.

Having made the decision to leave, our next dilemma was where to go, the United States or England. We decided on the latter because it made sense to live closer to Karen's family. There was one obstacle to putting our plan into immediate action, however. The Council had imposed a total ban on all Liberians leaving the country. Karen still had a British passport and citizenship, but it affected the children, who were born in the country, and, of course, me.

The intervention of the British Embassy in Monrovia, albeit after long delay and deliberation about our children, opened the gate to us leaving. Because they were minors, the children were placed on Karen's passport and Karen and the children flew out to England in June 1980, two months after the coup. I stayed behind, not knowing if or when things would change. Although I was married to a British citizen, I was still Liberian and the embassy in Monrovia was less concerned about my welfare.

Being on my own in a country where lawlessness and anomie was the order of the day was lonely and frightening. The constant presence of drunken, uneducated soldiers parading the streets with machine guns and sometimes firing their guns in the air indiscriminately was increasingly stressful. Although I was still able to go to work, the dusk-to-dawn curfew remained. The situation was such that nobody knew who to trust anymore, something reinforced as reports began circulating of missing people and bodies found on the beach simply because they were of the wrong tribe or of Americo-Liberia descent.

After a few months though, the imposed travel ban on Liberians leaving the country was relaxed, but only for educational purposes. Additionally, you were required to obtain travel clearance from the immigration office, which was controlled by the PRC. Based on my qualifications and contacts in England, I had no difficulty applying to and being accepted by a university in Sussex to pursue a course of study in management. This was merely my exit strategy as I had absolutely no intention at the time of studying. Obtaining the necessary clearances was difficult and involved offering bribes to officials in the immigration office. Eventually, however, I was granted a visa by the British Embassy, not just to study but also to 'join my family' in England.

The relaxation of the travel restrictions precipitated an exodus and a brain drain of many professional Liberians, including doctors, nurses, engineers, who had, years earlier, been encouraged to return in response to the Liberianisation policy. Five months after the coup, and three months after Karen and the children had left for England, I boarded a plane at Roberts International Airport for a night flight to London, without any of our possessions. Once again, I was leaving my parents, other family members and friends, this time in a period of uncertainty for those I left behind.

The check-in at the international airport in Liberia seemed to take twice as long on this particular night due to security checks. Soldiers with machine guns were everywhere, seeming to far outnumber the passengers. Although I had acquired all the right documents and clearances to leave the country, I was still fearful of being stopped and prevented from travelling. I also had in my possession a substantial sum in American dollars which I knew could be confiscated. I didn't want to imagine what would happen to me to if I were discovered leaving the country with such contraband. The atmosphere in the airport was tense, terrifying, especially so for me, knowing that I could be prevented from boarding the plane at any point.

Finally on board, I remained alert, unable to relax until we were airborne and well beyond Liberia's borders and airspace. My immediate reaction, to help me relax, was to request a glass of red wine and, after several such requests, I reclined in my seat. What seemed minutes later, although it had been an eight-hour flight, I awoke to the announcement that we were approaching Gatwick Airport and should prepare for landing.

Although I was arriving in England and feeling happy and looking forward to being reunited with Karen and the children, I also reflected on the five wonderful years we had had in Liberia and the sad manner in which our dream of living, working and bringing up our children there had ended. I also reflected on the safety of my family back in Liberia and wondered if we would ever meet any of them again.

PART 2

RETURNING TO ENGLAND

CHAPTER 5

Home away from home

DESPITE THE INCLEMENT WEATHER THAT MID-SEPTEMBER MORNING IN 1980, it was a great relief to land at Gatwick Airport and be met by the familiar figure of my father-in-law, Roy. It was five months after the military coup in Liberia and three months after Karen and the kids had left. Karen was not at the airport because the children, particularly Michael, would have been very upset if, for some reason, I had not made the flight. While going through immigration, I was made conscious of the fact that once again I was a foreigner. Despite carrying all the relevant documents, I had to answer many questions about my motives for being in the UK and how I was planning to support myself while in the country. Our drive back to Hastings was reminiscent of the original journey I had made seventeen years earlier, as a teenager.

The difference between now and seventeen years ago was that I was returning against my wishes and due to circumstances over which I had no control. As a Liberian I had reconnected with my roots and identity as a Liberian and now I felt that I was about to lose that sense of identity by returning to England. There is a truth to the local adage that once you come to Hastings, you never leave. I was back, not as a student or a visitor, which I had done many times before, but to establish a new home under very different circumstances. Unlike previous visits, which had been planned and organised, this one had been precipitated by events over which we had no control and which had threatened my safety. We had also had to leave all our possessions, savings and house in Liberia, as well as my friends and family.

It was understandably an emotional reunion with Karen and the children. Michael, who was four years old and too young to comprehend the situation, had been traumatised and distressed when I had not been able to travel to England with them. The joy on his face when we were reunited is stamped on my memory. His words were far simpler: 'Oh, hello'. Leaving Liberia without me appeared to have had a greater effect on him than we had imagined, despite our frequent communication during those three months apart. The words and emotions of a four-year-old who had not seen his dad for so long were hard. Karen told me that he had cried for me in the airplane as they left Liberia. Michelle was a baby and not obviously affected.

Prior to my arrival, Karen and the children had been in accommodation provided by Hastings Borough Council, in a building specifically for mothers and children, which meant I had to live with her parents. A few days after my arrival, the council moved us to a two-bedroom flat close to the Hastings town centre, just a few minutes' walk from the railway station. The condition of the flat was our awakening to the struggles and realities we would encounter in our efforts to re-establish ourselves. To say it was filthy would be an understatement. It was depressing, had no natural light and mainly consisted of a long corridor with a kitchen at the end and two small bedrooms projecting from one side of the corridor. We spent days cleaning up and trying to make it habitable but the depression never went away. The housing manager who took us to the flat must have seen our expressions of dismay when he led us into the flat and handed over the keys.

A week or so after we had moved in, we received an unexpected visit from the man; he wanted to see how we were settling in. He was visibly surprised at the cleanliness of the flat and the transformation we had made to it. We were contacted a few days later with the offer of a three-bedroom terrace house in a different part of the town, which we accepted. Public transport did not serve the area and for the first time in over ten years we did not own a car. The house was unfurnished and we had been forced to leave everything behind in Liberia. We were starting over yet again, but this time with two young children. The housing manager advised us to contact local charity shops and furniture warehouses. We didn't have the slightest clue about how or where to begin and what to say when we did. Luckily Karen's family helped.

Having sorted out our accommodation, I was now able to focus on my immigration status and to request the lifting of its restrictions. In my naïveté, I naturally assumed that being married to a British citizen and living in her country, I would be granted automatic entitlement to certain privileges like the freedom to seek employment in order to support my family. Yet, while Karen, as the spouse of a Liberian, was allowed to seek employment while there, the same privilege was not accorded me when I came to England as the spouse of a British citizen.

The consequences of not being allowed to work and the experience and humiliation of living on the 'dole' and having to 'sign-on' in order to receive state benefit and assistance for me were depressing. What was significant about this experience was the misuse of power and the attitude of the frontline staff at those agencies who were meant to help destitute people or those in need. It wasn't so much to do with having to receive money but more to do with the power and attitude of those who were charged with the responsibility of assessing my eligibility for entitlement of state benefit. I was treated as a number and often asked very personal questions about myself. Never was I accorded any respect, and no one seemed to want to believe my story of why and how we had to flee Liberia.

It was like an obstacle course dealing with these agencies. One of the frustrations we encountered with the benefit authority was their constant request for documents from my employer in Liberia, which I clearly could not produce because of the political situation. Despite repeatedly stating the situation in Liberia, I still detected some disbelief on their part as to why I could not produce my papers. They also seemed suspicious of the fact that I was married to a British subject who had also lived in Liberia. There was absolutely no sympathy for the fact that we had not only lost our house but had been unable to access my bank account because of the restrictions the military had imposed on financial institutions. I even sensed traces of suspiciousness over the fact that I was claiming to be married to a British citizen. I began to question whether our decision to return to England had been a mistake and whether we should, in fact, have returned to America.

Years later, I was able to reflect on this experience with a view to understanding what had actually happened. The frontline staff in those essential welfare agencies and authorities had no knowledge or understanding of what it was like for people fleeing atrocities and civil wars and being forced to come to England for safety. Even I did not understand what it meant for me as each day highlighted new challenges and experiences. I have enormous empathy for those who are regularly subjected to that type of treatment and my experiences in 1980, in those early months, paved the way to an understanding of how I would later respond to the needs of those who were disadvantaged and in need of an advocate.

Unlike those powerless citizens who frequented these services for assistance and were humiliated in the process, I was determined that my frustration and humiliation would be temporary. On the positive side, I experienced how generous the British public could be. We were warmly welcomed by our neighbours. Being the only interracial family on our close created obvious curiosity, yet a few of our neighbours came over and gave us blankets, curtains and other vital household items, which were appreciated even if the condition of some of the items was so poor that we were never able to use them. It was their thought and generosity that mattered.

In the end, the legal immigration process took more than ten months and involved having to secure the services of a solicitor to successfully facilitate my application to acquire British Resident status which accorded me certain privileges and entitlements, including the right to employment. During that period it was a good experience for me remaining at home and assisting with looking after the kids, especially as Michael had started at a school that wasn't too far from our home.

I was overwhelmed with joy when the Home Office finally granted me Permanent Residence status. I had not worked in almost a year and that had taken its toll on my pride, self-confidence and self-worth. That was all about to change. Now I could legitimately look for employment. It was a proud day for all of us, in November 1999, when I was granted UK citizenship.

CHAPTER 6

Beginning my
social work journey

SEEKING EMPLOYMENT BECAME BOTH MY FOCUS
AND PRIORITY. I hunted for work in the local job centre
and later extended my searches to the library, methodically
going through the papers and job adverts.

One day I came across an ad for a Residential Childcare
Worker at Old Roar House, a children's home, owned and
run by the local authority. As I read it, I was unsure what the
post entailed. I had no knowledge of social services and its
statutory duties in relation to the protection and welfare of
children. In West Africa, the practice of placing children in the
care of the local authority simply did not exist. Parents were

expected to care for their children and if they were unable to fulfil that parental duty for any reason, the responsibility fell to members of the extended family.

When I contacted them, I took up the offer of an informal visit, before returning to the library to begin my research on the British welfare system. The receptionist at the library recommended the 'Teach Yourself' book *Social Services Made Simple*, which I began to read and later purchased. It proved immensely valuable. I was also confident that my CV and degree, plus my experience of working on an adolescent psychiatric unit in America the summer camps, would stand me in good stead.

I gathered some relevant local history about Old Roar House. It was a red brick, four-floor Victorian building, located on two acres of land in St Leonards-on-Sea, a town adjoining Hastings. Prior to the 1970s, it had been a Barnado's Home, accommodating boys aged between five and sixteen, the latter the age I'd been when I first came to England. Old Roar was one of four local authority-run facilities for children in the Hastings area.

On the day of my informal meeting with the officer-in-charge (OIC), I woke up feeling determined, optimistic and keen to take my first steps towards a career in social work. I decided to make the two-and-a half-mile journey on foot. My arrival was announced by the OIC's dog. A few seconds after ringing the bell, a young teenager opened the door, clearly shocked at seeing a Black man on the threshold. Even so, he politely introduced himself, saying his name was Fred. When I indicated that I had an appointment, he said, 'Yes, he is expecting you' and escorted me to an office.

I was warmly greeted by William, the OIC, and his wife Tess, who worked at the home as a bursar-cum-deputy. I learned that there were fifteen all-white long-stay residents at Old Roar House and that the care workers were regarded by the residents as house parents. As a Black person, the thought of being referred to as a house parent by young white boys made me uncomfortable. The young lad who had greeted me at the door must have described me to the other residents, because within minutes of my arrival they all seemed to have a reason for walking past the door to see who I was and to offer us cups of tea.

There was something likeable and genuine about both William and Tess They were very welcoming and radiated warmth during their conversation with me about themselves, what their work entailed and their passion for wanting to make a difference to the young people at the home. They talked to me about a number of things including their Irish ancestry and their two teenage children, who lived with them at the home. They also talked about their childcare philosophy, social services generally and about the young people who lived at the home.

We talked for so long that I never had an opportunity to tour the building. I also discovered that the couple's knowledge was not limited to childcare issues alone. They also seemed to have had a good knowledge of world geography and history. When I mentioned my Liberian origin, William seemed to know about my country and its history. If I had to make a summary of this meeting, I would say that it went better and they were far more friendly than I had anticipated. We had an instant chemistry and friendship and although I was aware that they were probably granting similar visits and interviews to other interested applicants, I was glad to have met them, irrespective of what the outcome of the visit and formal interview. Like most people of their generation, they were still having to struggle with what I call 'nomenclature', or the appropriate choice of words when referring to people who were non-white. At times during our discussion, they seemed to use the words 'Black', 'coloured' and 'Negro', almost as though they were interchangeable. Still, I began my walk back home with very pleasant memories.

As part of the process for informal meetings, William was required to write his assessment of each prospective applicant, with a recommendation of how to proceed to his line manager.

A week after our meeting, I was invited for a formal interview and as I had anticipated, the OIC was on the interview panel, together with his line manager and a female officer from the personnel department. The fourth member of the panel, Len, was the assistant principal from Tile Barn, the children's centre.

Nothing of any significance stands out in my recollection of that interview except, as anticipated, the issue of race and ethnicity and the occasional struggles of some members of the panel with current terminology relating to people of colour. Having spent some years in America in the 1970s, when it was important at the time to get the wording right, I felt some somewhat uneasy hearing the words 'colour' and 'Negro' used interchangeably by an all-white interview panel some ten years later. I did also wonder whether the other candidates, who were all white, had been asked in their interviews whether the colour of their skin would be a barrier or hindrance to their ability to work with children and young people. Feeling powerless and also desperate to gain employment, I did not want to bite the potential hand that could feed me by challenging or educating the panel on race matters, particularly on the numerous generalities and assumptions about race and racism during that interview.

The following day, I received a phone call from the personnel office which was like the 'bad news and good news' story. First, the bad news. I was informed that the panel had felt and concluded that I was over-qualified for the post of care officer and therefore I could not be considered. Then the good news: I was told that Len Hammersley from Tile Barn had just advertised for an assistant group worker's post at the centre and based upon my qualifications and my interview performance, he had indicated that he was prepared to offer me that job with immediate effect, pending, of course, the usual references, police checks, etc. The personnel officer further indicated that if the post interested me then I should contact the assistant principal to arrange a meeting.

Without further hesitation, I telephoned Len. After a brief conversation, he invited me to visit the centre the next day. Tile Barn was a greater distance from home than Old

Roar, but I did not mind the walk. Len was a young and energetic-looking man who came across to me as a very nice guy. Unlike William at Old Roar, he had a social work qualification.

During our meeting, we revisited some of the issues discussed at the previous interview, including my professional views and philosophy on childcare, as well as the value he believed I would bring to the centre. It was good getting candid feedback from him on my performance during that interview and he explained to me the rationale behind the panel's decision about my appointment. He also felt that I was over-qualified for the assistant group worker's post that he was offering me, but urged me to consider it because of the career progression. He felt that I had the potential and qualifications to be a group leader at the centre. When he formally offered me the job, I accepted because of what he said about the possible progression and I was keen to get my foot in the door of the local authority, and, on 10 September 1981, my career with the local authority social services began.

Many years later, when employees were allowed to review their personnel records, my curiosity led me to request access to my own simply to see what information and documents the authority had on record. I couldn't help but grin when I came across the written feedback that William had sent to his manager following my informal visit at Old Roar. The first paragraph of the feedback memo began with the sentence: 'I was highly impressed with this *coloured gentleman*.'

Tile Barn was managed by a principal and two assistant principals. Each assistant principal was responsible for the management and day-to-day activities of a unit headed by a group leader with the support of several group workers and assistant group workers, of which I was now one. The principal had left prior to my appointment and the role was being shared by the two assistants. Education was provided on the premises for the majority of those residents who, for a variety of reasons, were unable to attend mainstream schooling.

There were significant differences in childcare practices and philosophy between a children's home and children's centre. The former was seen as a long-stay residence for young people, many of whom came to regard it as home. In contrast, a children's centre was for short placements and provided assessment prior to a move into either a substitute family or sheltered independent living. The qualifications of the staff in each differed significantly. 'House parents' in a children's home were mostly unqualified, whereas in a children's centre many held social work degrees or the Certificate in Social Services (CSS), which was the standard qualification for residential social workers. The staff at the centre were mostly qualified in comparison to the care staff in the children's home who were regarded by the residents as house parents.

My assessment of the staff in my unit, with two exceptions, was that they were pretty unfriendly and took great pride in being referred to by their job titles. In my first supervision meeting with the assistant principal he confirmed what I had already suspected: I was the first ever Black member of staff at the centre. He also hinted that my qualifications might be seen as a challenge to some of my colleagues and warned me about the possible racist attitude of some of the staff.

The two units seemed to have different unwritten philosophies and work ethics. Mine appeared *laissez-faire* and unstructured, and as a consequence, the young people lacked guidance and structure. They exploited those weaknesses and seemed to control the unit with negative and anti-social behaviour, in contrast to the other unit which seemed more organised and focused.

On my first evening shift, a male resident who had gone into town returned to the centre in a very aggressive state, heavily under the influence of alcohol. He proceeded to disrupt the calm atmosphere and to damage the furniture in the lounge where the other residents were quietly watching television. His aggressive behaviour soon spread to the other residents. The group leader in charge contacted Len. Following his arrival, Len secured himself in the office with the other staff to discuss what to do, leaving me to supervise the lounge.

So, there I was, my first week on the job, in the thick of it, with no induction programme or awareness of the centre's policies and procedures for dealing with this form of disturbed behaviour. I also had no knowledge of the young people I was being asked to supervise, while my three colleagues stayed in the office smoking and drinking coffee, under the cover of a 'strategy meeting'. Being Black rendered me a target for racist abuse from the disruptive resident, who was later joined by some of the others, who had hitherto been pleasant towards me. Calm was eventually restored when the lads responsible left the room. Nothing was resolved other than having to write a report of the incident.

Tile Barn operated on a daily two-shift system, morning and evening, with a waking officer at night. The staff also operated a rota for sleep-in duties. There was a handover meeting between shifts, with particular importance on the afternoon handover between the departing morning team and the arriving afternoon team. During this period, two staff members would be nominated by the group leader to supervise the residents, while the others were in the team room. I seemed to have had more than my share of supervising the residents during this period. However, from the few meetings I was selected to attend my observations were that they were very unprofessionally managed and merely an opportunity for the staff to congregate in a smoke-filled room for forty-five minutes to discuss the behaviour of residents with whom they had limited contact or interaction with during the shift. It was like a social gathering and, as a newcomer, I felt excluded, my professional assessment and input not valued nor sought for by the group leader.

I felt powerless and unable to offer any opinion or views during these handover meetings and that annoyed me for the simple reason that in comparison to others in the team I had spent most of the morning and evening shifts playing table tennis and football with the residents, getting to know them and some of their issues.

My opinion and evaluation of the assistant principal, who had greatly impressed me during my interview, soon began to wane. The culture and attitude in his unit, where I was based, was totally different from that of the other unit and the assistant principal responsible for the unit. As an assistant group worker, I tried in various subtle ways to bring energy and enthusiasm to the job, with limited success. The staff morale on the unit was hopelessly low. There was a lack of interest and commitment from both the group workers and the group leader.

The already low staff morale sank even further within a few weeks of my joining the centre when serious rumours, from reliable sources, began to circulate that the local authority was planning a restructuring of children's services which would result in the closure of Tile Barn and the redevelopment and upgrading of Old Roar House and the other two children's homes in the area. As what limited information available filtered down to the staff team, it seemed that despite the intervention of the union, the rumours would soon turn into reality. Less than a month into my employment, we were formally notified of the closure of the centre.

CHAPTER 7

Back to Old Roar House

WHILE THE TRADITIONAL APPROACH OF RESIDENTIAL CARE HOMES enabled children to remain in the care system until they reached eighteen, for many these homes failed to give them either the security or the experience of family life. We were told that the underlying basis for the restructuring of services was geared towards moving children from care homes either back with their biological parents or, failing that, with foster families. The local authority cited emerging evidence of the detrimental effects of long-term care and institutionalisation on children. The restructuring would mean that each resident would have a care plan and a period of professional assessment and preparation prior to discharge, leading to rehabilitation with their natural family or, when that plan wasn't achievable, with substitute foster carers.

News of the closure and restructuring of residential services for children across the county led to enormous staff anxiety, particularly with regard to job security. As a newcomer in the organisation I had limited knowledge of why these changes were being proposed. I found it difficult to show or express genuine empathy with my colleagues who, I became aware, were having informal meetings among themselves from which I had deliberately been excluded. We were also assured that there would be no redundancies and that displaced staff would be redeployed. To add to the uncertainty, Tile Barn's assistant principal, the man who appointed me, suddenly announced his departure.

Following a lengthy period of consultation, we received more unwelcome news regarding the process of closure and redeployment. With the restructuring and upgrading of the home to a centre all staff must reapply for their jobs or any vacant posts within the new structure. We were told that personnel would set up a process, again in consultation with the union, towards the successful achievements of these objectives.

I felt particularly vulnerable because of my probationary status. All staff members were instructed to use up all their accrued overtime and annual leave and staff from establishments would cover for those on leave. Not having accrued any overtime or leave entitlement, I was the first to be asked to work alternate shifts between the centre and another home which had also been earmarked for closure.

Most of the residents at this particular home were

pre-teenagers and very institutionalised, having lived in the home for so long. The residential care staff were very caring and, like Old Roar House, were seen as 'house parents'. In many ways I enjoyed the experience of alternating between the centre and the home, not only because the latter was closer to where I lived but also because I felt more accepted by the staff and residents. It was a joy taking these young kids out for walks and engaging them in social activities. I learned that the officer-in-charge of the home had requested retirement.

Eventually the new posts in the upgraded Old Roar House were advertised. These included three group leaders, several group workers and a team of assistant group workers. There seemed to have been the natural assumption among my colleagues at Tile Barn that everybody would reapply for their current jobs and that I, being an assistant group worker, would reapply for the same post. However, I reflected on what the assistant principal had said to me at my appointment and his prediction that I would go further. Having seen what each job entailed, and after carefully reading the specifications for the three different positions, I took a few days to consider my decision. In the end, and with a degree of confidence and optimism, I decided to apply for the one of the three group leader posts.

When the news of my application became common knowledge, I sensed immediate animosity. Most of my colleagues adopted the silent treatment. Sadly, there was no one I trusted enough to talk to at work and the assistant principal had already informed the team of his departure. I did, however, find someone with whom I could have general conversations. He was one of the group workers who had befriended me and was in the final year of CSS training. He often gave me a ride home at night because he was concerned for my safety walking through the estate that led to Tile Barn. The only other friend I had at work was another group worker who was also planning to enrol for her CSS training in the following year.

The animosity intensified when my colleagues learned that I had been shortlisted and invited to attend an interview. Meanwhile, William, the officer in charge at Old Roar House, had already been promoted to principal and I was aware that he would be on my interview panel. Other members included a personnel officer, the team manager (line manager to the principal) and the area manager, who was well-known as a no-nonsense, straight-talking man with a powerful image and presence. Some colleagues regarded him as intimidating because of his very macho style of management, which at the time reflected the culture of the organisation. The word was that he was one of those managers you instantly either liked or disliked.

Preparing for the interview, I reminded myself of the fact that at that time in England and particularly in East Sussex, Black people were under-represented in the supportive areas of social care. We were typically assigned stereotypical roles like domestic workers or carers in homes for the elderly. I wanted to change that and make a difference by cracking the glass ceiling.

In contrast with my earlier experience, the interview went

well and was conducted in a professional manner. Unlike today, panel members were at liberty to ask candidates questions now deemed prejudicial. As I had expected, they started by asking me about race and culture. Once we got past those 'Where are you from?' and 'Where are you *really* from?' – questions still regularly asked today – the focus of the interview turned to the job specification and my ability to lead a team. I felt confident and pleased at the end of the process.

Later that evening, I received a phone call from personnel offering me the post of group leader, which I was delighted to accept. I was told that the two existing group leaders at Tile Barn had lost their posts and would be downgraded. The OIC of one of the homes marked for closure became the second group leader; the third vacancy was later filled externally.

I was sensitive to the feelings of the staff group and what to expect from them when I walked into the staff room the following morning. You could have heard a pin drop. I read the body language and saw the expression on the faces of those in the room. Obviously, there would be no congratulations. I had to deliberately suppress my excitement at my promotion so as not to appear arrogant and unsympathetic. I was particularly aware that as group leader, the composition of my team was bound to include a number of these present in the staff room.

Reliable sources later informed me that some members of the staff team had described my appointment as 'tokenism', that I was chosen as a symbolic Black man and not promoted in management because of my qualifications. I was under no illusion that from that moment on my professional skills and ability would be under the microscope. My experience of racism had taught me that in order to be given average consideration as a Black man and professional, I had to be better than average both skills-wise and intellectually in order to be given average consideration. Ironically, I would be returning to Old Roar, albeit in a different role from that in which I had initially intended to work. I was looking forward to the new challenges and opportunities in the new centre. I was particularly pleased to be given the opportunity of working with the principal and his wife, who had remained as bursar.

Within four months of getting my foot in the door of the local authority, I had risen from assistant group worker to group leader. This was a remarkable achievement; I had raised the glass ceiling. I was happy to return to where I started with an informal visit and first interview. The home was now a centre and I was now the leader of a team that comprised colleagues who had been my seniors only a few weeks earlier. The days ahead would present numerous challenges and adjustments for all of us.

The new principal had lost all of his original team of loyal house parents and inherited some very disgruntled staff, particularly from Tile Barn. Morale was low and it was an uncomfortable time for all of us in this testing atmosphere with its awkward dynamics. I had to find a way to lead a team.

The first six months of the life in the new centre was a challenging period for all of us, particularly the principal, who had been accustomed to a free reign. He had to adapt and compromise his traditional beliefs and childcare principles to the aims and objectives of the new regime. He also had the arduous task of bringing together a team of qualified staff who were unhappy, demotivated and struggling to embrace the new order. Although the principal regarded himself as a good and fair disciplinarian with years of experience in youth work, his situation was compromised by the simple fact that he did not have a recognised qualification in social work or residential social work. Some of his staff had these, and consequently his childcare philosophy came under increasing scrutiny and analysis.

Despite me having built up a good working relationship the principal, we often found ourselves agreeing to disagree on matters relating to childcare. I was determined to remain loyal to him. Unlike some of my colleagues, I did not dismiss all his ideas, for they had achieved positive results for some of the young people. My loyalty and gratitude to him and his wife became a personal one. Immediately following my appointment as group leader, my baby daughter was admitted to hospital with pneumonia. My wife and I spent long periods at the hospital and, knowing that we did not have a car, the principal regularly took me to the hospital for an hour during the working day. This act of kindness and practical assistance lasted nearly a week, far surpassing my expectations. I felt I owed him and his wife my loyalty and support during their difficult honeymoon period at the new centre.

As I settled into my new role in the new regime, I wondered how the local authority planned to achieve its statutory duties and responsibilities in respect of its vulnerable young clients. I had gleaned some insight during my interview and understood the theoretical framework which underpinned the changes. In the early 1980s, the concept of evidence-based practice was beginning to drive social work intervention and was reflected in the emerging professional approach assessing and working with teenagers to working with and assessing the needs of vulnerable teenagers.

As a student, one of my course modules had been about child and adolescent development and psychology. During that period, I became fascinated with the work of G. Stanley Hall, the pioneering American psychologist whose focus was on childhood development. Hall identified that the adolescent period was one of heightened 'storm and stress' during which most teenagers were in conflict with their parents, were moody and engaged in risky behaviour. He asserted that most of the stress was related to a lack of identity and peer pressure; school had an important influence during that period. A few years later, I became inspired and influenced by Eric Erickson, the German-born American psychologist and psychoanalyst, and his theory on the stages of psychosocial development and his work on identity crisis.

Having this theoretical knowledge and foundation were relevant in facilitating my work at Old Roar. These theories resonated in my work at the centre: most of our adolescent clients were there because of problems in their families which had negatively affected their social development and education. I could see that their behaviour was driven by peer pressure and other issues identified by Stanley Hall. The local authority's strategy for helping these young people presented a challenging task for any social worker working with adolescents during that period. If the adolescent period is known to be difficult even for the 'normal' adolescent, it is inevitably more difficult, traumatic and challenging for young people in the residential care system. The phrase 'children in need' is defined in law as children who are under eighteen years of age and deemed to be in need of local authority services in order to achieve or maintain a reasonable standard of health and development.

The primary aim of the centre was to assess the individual needs of our young clients and to formulate a long-term placement plan incorporating appropriate interventions. My role as group leader was to ensure that my team were effectively engaging with the young people in order to assess their needs. Unfortunately, it took some months of unnecessary distractions before we could focus on our task and responsibilities.

Despite having a high calibre of qualified childcare staff, we struggled with personality clashes and teething problems with the management system. One major difficulty, as I perceived it, was that the new principal, who had previously and successfully run a long-stay children home with his team of loyal house parents, found it difficult to 'let go' and delegate work to his three group leaders. Instead, he tried to micro-manage all activities within the centre, wanting to be seen by the residents as the only person with power and authority. I sensed that he felt challenged by his team and by our qualifications, which led to him undermining our authority. This often resulted in conflict.

I experienced this after a weekend when, as the group leader in charge of the centre, I had allowed some of the residents to go to the cinema on the Sunday afternoon as a reward for good behaviour. We were always aware that historically a number of the domestic staff would habitually contact the principal at home to inform him of what was happening at the centre. That Monday morning the principal arrived at the centre during the residents' breakfast. Noticing that one particular resident had not yet arrived in the dining room, he summoned the lad to his office. Within about five minutes I was also called to the office and, as I entered, he immediately began to question my motive for allowing the resident to go to the cinema. I told him quite firmly that if he wanted my reason, I was happy and prepared to give it, but not in the presence of the resident. His agenda was clearly to humiliate me in front of the resident in order to demonstrate that he had ultimate power and control, including over his group leaders.

He became so concerned about losing his authority that he no longer took holidays and, on his weekends off, he often found reasons to 'pop back' to the centre. Despite some professional differences though, we had mutual trust and respect for each other and because of that I always tried to make myself available to talk to him about his style of management. I felt he did appreciate the advice I gave him, although it did not change his style.

Focusing on my professional role and duties, I found

working with some of young people both rewarding and personally challenging, rewarding in that I felt we did try to make a difference in the lives of the majority of the residents by providing them the stability they perhaps never experienced. It was also challenging in that we were frequently on the receiving end of their frustrations, aggression and anti-social behaviour. Occasionally, they tried to justify and rationalise their behaviour by informing us that we did not understand them because our background experiences were different from theirs and that we represented the authority responsible for making decisions about their care and welfare. I did get the feeling that as I was Black and from a minority group, they identified with me and perhaps felt we had something in common. At times I felt able to connect with these young people where others struggled to do so.

Due to a lack of stability and positive role models in their formative years, we could see the effects on the emotional and psychological development of some of these young people. This resulted in an inability to form trusting relationships; education was positively rewarding.

Weekend shifts were often the most difficult ones as these shifts often brought out the most unpredictable behaviour, particularly when combined with drinking alcohol and sniffing glue. With or without permission, it was not unusual for some of the residents to go to town and fail to return to the centre at the expected time or not to return at all. When this happened the leader on the shift was required to notify the police that the young person was either 'missing' or had 'failed to return'.

Depending on the time of night and the vulnerability of the individual, the police would sometimes arrive at the centre to collect details and a description of the missing teenager. When the police officer arrived, they would inevitably request to speak to the officer-in-charge and I always enjoyed watching the expression on their faces when I told them I was the team leader in charge. On one occasion, the officer tried to make conversation with me by asking how I, a Black person, was treated by the residents. My spontaneous reply was that they treated me at times no differently from the way they treated the police, and that it wasn't about race or racism but their rebellion against power and authority.

My memories and experiences as group leader varied from the pleasant to the disastrous. Two examples of the latter stand out. The first was a planned and well-organised summer camping holiday with the male residents from the centre. This was in keeping with the principal's traditional theories: that camping was a male passion and activity.

The campsite was sixty miles away, close to a popular seaside resort. The residents may have seen this as a treat but I think the principal's motives had more to do with keeping them out of town that summer to prevent them from shoplifting and engaging in other anti-social behaviour. The arrangement was for two male staff members from each of the teams to spend alternate weeks on the campsite with the lads. That meant extra chores and responsibilities and having to spend a week working as well as cooking and preparing meals for ten youngsters. However, we took consolation from the assurance that we would be paid for the additional hours.

My assistant group worker and I were selected for the first week of the holiday. On the morning of our departure, we were all seated in the mini bus waiting to leave the centre when the principal arrived to inform us, in the presence of the residents, that the management had decided they would not pay overtime or give us time-off in lieu to compensate for the additional hours we would be working. He stated that we could cancel the trip if we did not agree with the decision. This was another power-wielding play, emotionally blackmailing us in the knowledge that at that late hour we would find it practically impossible to disappoint the lads who were looking forward to the holiday.

On our third day at camp, my assistant worker and I decided to give the youngsters a treat by going to Butlin's amusement resort, which was about 20 miles from our campsite. Upon arrival we set a time at which to meet the group at the car park for the journey back to the campsite. The lads set off in different directions to enjoy the various amusements, rides and activities.

A few hours into our visit, my colleague and I decided to have a stroll back in the vicinity where we had parked the minibus. As we were approaching, we noticed something unusual: a side window was missing and as we got nearer it was obvious that it had been smashed. The car park attendant informed us that three of 'your lads' had returned to the bus shortly after our arrival and broken it. He did not take any action because he said the lads were part of our group. It seemed that these residents had figured out that we had hidden all the holiday spending money somewhere in the minibus. They had located the cash box, smashed it open and left it empty on the seat of the minibus. With the holiday money in their possession, they had left the resort and headed to the town centre.

I immediately contacted the police to report the theft, the criminal damage and the three missing lads. The memorable moment for me came when the police arrived. I had been aware since our arrival that there were no other Black faces to be seen. Now here I was, the only Black man at the resort, seated in the back seat of a police car, next to a minibus with a smashed window, being questioned by the police. A crowd of curious holidaymakers had gathered and one did not have to be a genius to figure out what assumptions were being made. I felt embarrassed and self-conscious, and it was one of the rare occasions when I wished for the ground to open beneath my feet and swallow me. I felt like shouting out to the onlookers that I was not the guilty one. These were feelings that I could not share with my professional white colleagues.

As a Black professional in the early 1980s you often had to suffer in silence and not share your experiences for fear of being labelled 'too sensitive' or 'having a chip on your shoulder' or that you 'needed to be rescued' because you could not cope. Fearing all of these labels, you learn to suffer in silence.

Later that night, the three residents were returned to the campsite by the police who had found them loitering in town. Most of the stolen money had been used to purchase solvents and alcohol. The next day involved spending several hours at the local police station in the area where the residents had to make statements. As the person in charge, I had to make the difficult decision on behalf of the local authority as to whether the residents, who were in authority care, should be charged with theft and criminal damage. I decided that they should, which meant possible criticism when we returned to the centre.

Although I was glad to be back at the centre after the week away, I was angry that we had not been rewarded financially or with time-off in lieu. I felt powerless and did not take the matter any further with the principal. Towards the end of the summer, cracks were beginning to appear in the structure and management of the centre, manifesting themselves in a number of ways. Where previously staff were prepared to go the extra mile for the benefit of the residents, that was no longer happening; instead the staff sickness rate began to rise, particularly at weekends. Staff meetings had become increasingly divisive. Irrespective of all that, the principal continued to receive support from both his line manager and the operations manager. I began to seriously consider my own role within the management structure.

I felt that I had developed sufficient trust and respect from the principal to share my thoughts and assessment of the issues. In my next supervision session with him, I decided to focus on internal challenges and how they could be resolved. First and foremost, I felt that a deputy principal was needed to relieve the principal of some of the day-to-day demands and stresses of running the centre. What I felt unable to say was that I believed the problems were partly due to his management style of wanting to micro-manage the centre and failing to delegate. He genuinely appreciated my honesty and advice and indicated that he had taken them on board. I knew he did from the supervision recording of that meeting. Extracts from his recording read:

> *James expressed his feelings about support to me. He pointed out that there was a need for a deputy and until that comes, he was willing to do anything to help out. I thanked him and suggested that during my forthcoming absences (leave and courses) he would be in charge. He also expressed again his desire to get on the Certificate of Social Services (CSS) course.*

– Supervision record, March 1983

So he had taken my advice on board and shared it, albeit as his own idea, with his manager.

Within a few weeks, the new post of deputy principal was advertised. The principal was very keen to have me work as his deputy and, acting on his recommendation and encouragement I applied. The following week, I was notified that I had been shortlisted and therefore invited to attend an interview. I was aware that a number of external candidates had also been shortlisted.

I remained acutely conscious of the organisational glass ceiling. Being shortlisted for such a position in a predominantly white organisation made me aware of who I was and what I wanted to achieve. I was under no illusion about what this meant. Any attempt to crack this invisible barrier would be challenging and painful and was likely to raise personal issues about my identity and conformity. Fearing new challenges was never part of my nature, however, and at that stage and junction in my life and career I was confident about my identity as a Black man and did not need to conform to the identity imposed on me by my predominantly white organisation. I felt proud reflecting on the fact that within less than eight months of joining the local authority and having to start at the bottom, I was now applying for a manager's post. As I anticipated, there were negative reactions and comments from some colleagues who were still coming to terms with what they saw as my meteoric career rise and determination to continue rising. Through personal reflection and development, I was confident enough to ignore or dismiss such negativity.

I prepared for and approached the interview with the assumption that the process would not be conducted on an equal opportunity or level playing field basis. The organisational culture in those days was such that those on interview panels felt at liberty to ask candidates any questions they liked and, in some cases, to simply embarrass the candidate. For instance, women candidates were regularly asked about their childcare commitments, while Black candidates expected questions on race. The interview panel included the principal, his line manager, the area manager and a representative from personnel.

Less than fifteen minutes into the interview the panel abandoned their formal script about the job requirement and specifications vis-à-vis my suitability in favour of their traditional, uncomfortable script. The most senior member of the panel wanted to know what the issues were for me, 'a Black person, managing a team of white staff'. While I did not want to jeopardise my chances of promotion and the financial benefits for my family, I felt I needed to respond directly to this question. I did so in the form of another question to the panel: why did they feel managing a team of white staff had to be an issue for me? As an immediate follow-up, I politely asked whether they or my all-white colleagues saw my management of them as an issue. I then made it clear that my being Black was certainly not an issue for me. As expected, neither of my questions were responded to; instead, they quickly tried to steer the agenda and questions in another direction. I imagine what they wanted was for me to admit to vulnerabilities and fears so that they might be seen as 'rescuers,' out to help me deal with what they thought would be problems for me.

As the saying goes 'you don't bite the hand that feeds you' and at that stage in the interview I feared I may have done just that by challenging the panel. At the same time, I felt proud that I was able to challenge some of their perceptions and stereotypes. I was aware that several other candidates, all white, were also being interviewed that day and I couldn't help but wonder whether the issue of their race and ethnicity had featured in the process.

Later that evening, I received the much-anticipated phone call from personnel and the news was that my interview had been successful and that the panel had agreed to offer me the position of deputy principal. I had now cracked the glass ceiling at a higher level. Overjoyed, I spent the evening celebrating with my wife, Karen, and a bottle of wine and looking forward to starting in my new role.

Unfortunately, for me the celebration was premature. The following morning, I received another phone call from the same personnel officer informing me of a consultation meeting held later that evening. They had concluded that, as a result of not receiving many applications, the post would be re-advertised. In what was meant to be seen by me as a gesture of goodwill, she indicated that I would not need to reapply. Instead, I would automatically be shortlisted for the next interview.

I was angry and perplexed, and did not have time to digest or make sense of the new information I had received. In my anger, I reminded the personnel officer that 'they' must have all been aware of the number of applicants during shortlisting and when candidates were being invited for interview. I quickly realised that she was only the bearer of bad news and that as a personnel officer she was not party to the decision. What followed was perhaps one of the quickest career decisions I have ever made: I ended the conversation by indicating that I did not intend to be part of another interview process.

Without a doubt, the issue of my race had been a salient feature in both the interview process and the subsequent change of decision. This was a classic example of an institutional glass ceiling keeping a candidate from a higher position purely on the basis of a demographic characteristic. Sadly, there was no one I could talk to about my feelings. I lacked strategies and experience for dealing with situations of this kind. It left me feeling very isolated and facing the fact that I would have to continue working with the same players who had made the decision.

Yes, I was disappointed at not being appointed to the post, but I was more hurt by the way the decision was made. Nevertheless, I was determined not to let this setback and experience affect my aspirations and determination in furthering my career. What surprised me the most was that no one from the senior management team who was on the panel had the decency to meet with me afterwards to ask why I had withdrawn and how I was coping.

I believed in the expression 'nothing happens before its time', and in every setback I have experienced I have always tended to look for positives. In this particular instance, I rationalised what had happened by reminding myself of the fact that I had not long completed my six months' probationary period with the organisation and that it was a credit to me to have risen through the ranks to a position where I had been short-listed for deputy principal. I also saw it as an awakening or a reality check.

I was aware that even though I had a degree, I did not hold the standard recognised qualification in residential social work, the CSS. I came to the conclusion that in order to advance further I needed to obtain this qualification.

I was offered a place on the Sussex CSS scheme to pursue the two-year part-time training, beginning in early 1984. I continued on in my role as group leader at Old Roar. Following my unpleasant experience of the recruitment process and prior to the start of my CSS course, I was keen to learn about and do some research into race issues and race relations in England, including Black people's contribution to the society, real and perceived. Although I was aware of some of these issues and historic events. I had not put them into any meaningful context or perspective prior to my recent experience.

The story which fascinated me the most was the Bristol bus boycott of 1963, the very year I first arrived as a young boy in England. The boycott was led by Paul Stevenson, an Afro-Caribbean youth worker. The, Bristol Omnibus Company (BOC) had refused to employ Black or Asian crew in the city. A young man named Guy Reid-Bailey, who had come to England from Jamaica and settled in Bristol, wanted to work on the buses. Stevenson checked that there were vacancies and that the qualifications that Guy had were good enough. He arranged an interview for Guy and when the interview had been confirmed, he phoned the bus company to inform them that Guy was Afro-Caribbean. The company reacted by cancelling it. When Stevenson met with the general manager of the company to discuss the cancellation, he was told in no uncertain terms that the company did not employ Black staff on the buses.

In response Stevenson and Guy mobilised and organised people in Bristol to boycott the buses. This was effective in that all Bristolians, white and Black, refused to use the buses, gaining national and international media coverage. Finally, in August 1963, the bus company was forced to change its employment policy. Stevenson continued to campaign against racism in other areas. As a consequence of his movement, the first Race Relations Act was passed in 1965, followed by another in 1976. Both acts were based on the clear acknowledgement that racism existed in England and that Acts of Parliament were needed to address the racism in service delivery and in goods and services. Prior to reading about the Bristol bus boycott, I had been vaguely aware of the negative experiences of Black immigrants who started arriving from the Caribbean on SS *Windrush* in 1948. This continued over several decades, and extended to other ethnic minorities, including the British Asians expelled from Uganda by Idi Amin and the response to their arrival in England.

It was therefore a surprise to me to find when I started my CSS training that the programme had failed to incorporate issues of immigration and racism. One reason for this had to do with the social work movement of the late 1960s and early 1970s, which highlighted the class struggle in Britain while failing to engage with racism and the experiences of Black people, despite the emerging legal framework. Social work training was still failing to address issues of inequalities and social justice. The profession was seen by many as a middle-class one, unattractive to Black people.

However, the CSS did enlighten me on how the welfare system in the United Kingdom had evolved. In view of the fact that I was already managing a team, I particularly enjoyed and benefitted from the final-year specialist option, which was about management. It was challenging at times being a part-time group leader while doing a part-time course and having study days away from the centre.

During the management module, I again began to look at my career path and what I wanted to pursue after completing the course. Before the final option was finished, I had more or less made up my mind that I needed to move in a new and different direction from residential social work. Happily, I gained my CSS and resumed my full-time duties and responsibilities as group leader at Old Roar, feeling more confident now that I had acquired my professional qualification as a social worker.

Residential social work with young people had not been without its criticisms, not only because of the complexities of dilemmas and challenges it presents but also the unsociable working days and hours. That aside, I discovered that there were numerous benefits and rewards in that arena of the profession. For instance, the staff support and cohesion among the staff, particularly at difficult times, were second to none. Residential social workers did make a difference in the lives of many disadvantaged young people by providing them with the security and nurturing they had never experienced.

Most of them had entered the care system without having any social or moral boundaries and they had been stigmatised and labelled by most people as being beyond control. I was generally successful in being able to build a good relationship with these young people and I think they saw my sincerity towards them. I also grew to understand that when they became frustrated or angry with the world or authority, they tended to pick an obvious target for their catharsis. In Old Roar, this could be Black people and, at times, female staff who were frequently targets of very personal abuse.

Looking back on to those days and my interventions and engagement with teenagers, I can honestly say it was a great learning experience and I made many good friends. However, I was aware that the unsociable working hours and shifts were keeping me away from my own young children and family at the time when my own kids needed a daddy at home, particularly at weekends.

The last straw for me came on a Sunday afternoon when I returned home extremely exhausted after completing back-to-back shift (3 p.m.–11 p.m. and 7.30 a.m.–3 p.m.). My son came and asked me to take him to the park for football and I responded by saying that I was too tired. Having spent two shifts motivating and interacting with other children I had no energy to meet the needs of my own son. When I realised what I had said, I could not forgive myself and, as a result, I concluded that it was time to leave residential social work.

My personal decision to leave was eclipsed by another unfortunate but memorable event: our union was recommending industrial action because of low pay and unsociable working hours. Our area manager's approach to this proved ruthless and divisive. Instead of appealing to us collectively for our goodwill and understanding not to act because of the consequences for the residents in our care, he had all the staff assemble in the principal's office and without any greetings or preamble proceeded to ask us individually if we were planning to take industrial action. Where the answer was 'yes', he instructed the person to leave the room and the building to begin their strike. His bullying and intimidation caused some people who had planned to take industrial action to suddenly change their minds and turn their anger against their striking colleagues.

Instead of the help and guidance one might expect from a senior manager, the meeting divided the staff and further lowered the morale of the team. For a few of us, including the three group leaders, who stuck to our guns and did not strike, life was fine afterwards, but not for those who chose industrial action. Their careers in residential care were short-lived. As group leader, I had already made it clear to my team that while I was not going on strike, I would respect the decision of those who had decided to do so.

CHAPTER 8

When opportunity knocks

THE THEORETICAL BASIS FOR REPLACING LONG-
TERM PLACEMENTS in children's homes was sound. There
was a need to develop infrastructure; assessment, fostering and
sheltered accommodations. This proposal presented challenges
to the children, especially the older 'hard-to-place' children.
These centres had been their homes for many years and had
provided them with the stability and security they would not
have had otherwise. Whatever the options were, the facilities
simply didn't exist at the time.

The plan for an outreach team coincided with the completion of my CSS training. Along with my qualification,
I felt I had gained enough experience of residential social
work and staff management to enable me to move on in a

different direction. I was interested in the new theory and the opportunity it offered to bring my own vision to developing a team.

The outreach team was being set up as a two-year project to achieve a number of objectives. First and foremost was the task of recruiting, training and supporting substitute carers for teenagers who had spent years in residential care. Recruitment would be an ongoing team activity in order to develop and maintain a reserve of carers. The second task was to recruit, train and manage a pool of dedicated sessional workers to work with the families and children at home or in placements in order to prevent a breakdown.

When the new post was advertised, I did not hesitate to submit my application. I was shortlisted, interviewed and appointed to manage the new team. This would be my first independent test and challenge in managing a team and its resources. As a Black man, I was aware that I would need to convince or demonstrate to others that my promotion had not been based on tokenism. I was also aware that I would need to demonstrate that I merited the opportunity to manage a team of white people.

Disappointingly, I had no input into the selection of the five group workers who were appointed to the outreach team. I was aware that two of the workers were qualified residential social workers, while the remaining three were field social workers who had been redeployed from other teams. I was unsure of the circumstances that had led to their redeployment. One of the workers made no attempt to disguise his unhappiness. I gained the impression that the unhappiness had less to do with the circumstances and more to do with issues relating to me as his group leader. At that time there was a clear divide in the training and status between the qualifications for field social workers, the certificate of qualification in social work, CQSW, and for residential social workers, the CSS. The latter seemed to carry less status and recognition within the organisation. Whereas the holders of CQSW were eligible to work as residential social workers, holders of the CSS, like me, could not work as or perform field social work duties.

My first challenge was to deal with this disgruntled team member who had refused to become a team player and was determined to undermine my authority and destroy the team in its infancy. It proved a struggle trying to show empathy while also preventing him from damaging the morale and objectives of the team. Fortunately, after a few months, he decided to leave the team and the organisation. There was no delay in filling the vacant post with another CSS-qualified worker who brought new energy and ideas to the team. Throughout this period, I received helpful support and guidance from my new line manager.

The team and I embarked on our primary objectives. Most of these young people in the care system had experienced multiple placement breakdowns. The main reason for this was that the foster carers who had been tasked with looking after these teenagers were not properly informed of the nature of their problems and were not adequately trained and supported.

Recruitment of foster or substitute carers would be a long and ongoing activity in order to build up a pool of potential carers that was large enough to prevent the crises that led to residential care.

During those early weeks and months of setting up and defining the team, my new manager was very supportive. His guidance in our team building was invaluable particularly in helping us to agree on and set out our objectives and a schedule for achieving them. We identified the skills within the team and allocated responsibilities on that basis. As a fledgling team, we believed that in order to succeed we needed to break away from the traditional way of recruiting foster carers and to change the way they were perceived by the local authority. We felt it was essential to work with and treat our carers as professionals who would be providing a valuable service to the authority and that they should be paid accordingly. A traditional assumption about foster carers was that they did the job not for money but because they loved working with children. We advocated that fostering should be seen as a career and that foster or substitute carers deserved respect. The team and I were determined that our recruitment campaigns would not be limited exclusively to targeting white, middle-class married couples. We wanted a broader appeal that reflected our client group.

When the local media became aware of the specialist team and what it was aiming to achieve, we were inundated with requests to facilitate in advertising and promoting our recruitment campaigns at no cost to the local authority. I was aware of the fact that statutory organisations had rigid sets of procedures and protocols for communicating with the media. Following the rules worked out fairly well for our first campaign, but after that we began to encounter problems. The media had deadlines for articles awaiting publication and I was increasingly frustrated when we missed a deadline because what we were hoping to publicise had not been approved by the necessary department or manager.

Failure to adhere to this rigid and bureaucratic policy was my first major challenge, that and confronting my line manager and the authority. Having planned a new recruitment drive for approved providers of sheltered accommodations, I waited several days for a decision from the necessary department in the organisation. With the clock ticking, I decided to take the risk of giving the newspaper permission to proceed with the publication, hoping that approval would be granted before the article was in print. Unfortunately, things turned out differently and I was read the riot act by my manager, even though publication brought successful outcomes. I have always believed in taking risks and have no regrets in bypassing line management and the slow machinery of the authority.

The response to these campaigns exceeded expectations. Given that the authority already had an existing fostering and adoption team, the agreed arrangement was that the outreach team would recruit and train all the new foster carers. They would then be transferred to the fostering team for ongoing support. I did not favour this arrangement because I felt that the existing fostering and adoption team had demonstrated that they were unable to provide the level of support that some carers needed. However, I had to understand and accept the fact that the outreach had been set up as a two-year project and a longer-term arrangement was necessary.

Social workers and the social work profession have often been portrayed as politically correct and too liberal with respect to social issues, particularly those relating to diversity, race and culture. The 1970s brought into consciousness the disproportionately high number of Black children in residential care who had also been labelled and stigmatised as 'hard to place', and the debate that was being had in local authorities was the appropriateness of transcultural adoption and fostering. In essence, that meant the fostering or adoption of Black children by white families and not the fostering of white children by Black carers.

As a West African, I was reminded of my own history and journey to England for education in the early 1960s, although I had a privileged experience at a boarding school. I was still able to understand the reasons why families from other West Africans countries sent their children to England. Whereas I had left England after my studies, many other West Africans chose to remain, for a number of reasons, including cultural. Because of economic and social issues, the disproportionality of Black children in the care of the local authorities was a result of some families being unable to provide care. There was also the common practice of West African parents putting their children into private foster care while the parents continued with their own education. As a social worker, I worked with several British families in my area who were looking after African children who had not had contact with their natural family for years and therefore had to call on the local authority for help.

The care and welfare of Black children tended to divide opinion among social work professionals. On one side of the debate were those who believed that Black children should only be fostered or adopted by Black families because only Black people understood their needs and therefore could better provide them with a sense of identity. In the absence of such families, however, these young Black kids should remain in residential care. On the other side were those who believed that Black children could be fostered by white carers if they were appropriately trained and were able to recognise racial differences and thereby to help Black children in care celebrate these differences.

As a Black social worker, I would not remain unaffected by the nature of the debate. At the time, I was aware of the Soul Kids Campaign in London in 1975.which was the first attempt in England to address and remedy the issue by specifically recruiting Black families to care for Black children. Equipped with the knowledge and outcome of this campaign, as my profile began to grow, I began to play a valuable role in giving guidance and advice to colleagues who were struggling with the dilemma of transracial fostering and adoption in their practice. An assumption frequently made by some in relation to such problems naturally boiled down to race. No such analysis and conclusions were made about white carers who looked after white children.

I frequently received phone calls from social workers asking for advice and intervention with foster families who cared for Black teenagers. I regularly had to challenge and dispel the notion and assumption that because the placement was a transracial one, the problems must inevitably relate to racial issues. I found myself pointing out that many of the difficulties were from rejection, neglect and a consequent inability to sustain relationships with adults. Race was a red herring. Some of those difficulties in those teenagers' lives had been compounded or precipitated by the onset of adolescence.

The first such client who I encountered was Fatu, a teenage girl who had been brought to England from West Africa by her parents. They placed her in private foster care with a religious single white woman while they pursued their university education. The difficulty was that the girl was simply abandoned by her parents; when the carer encountered serious difficulties and could no longer manage the emerging teenager, the young girl was removed by the local authority and placed in residential care. In my daily encounters with her, the issue which stood out most was her denial of her Blackness and frequent emphatic claim that her complexion was lighter than mine. Eventually, I was able to build a good, trusting relationship with her, discussing Africa and African literature to help her develop and be proud of her heritage. She began to see me as a role model and to form an attachment to me. I felt particularly sad when the Home Office, having traced her maternal grandparents, deported her to Nigeria.

A similar case concerned a white foster family who had looked after three West African brothers under the same arrangement as that of the African girl. The two elder boys excelled in school and, after reaching adulthood, moved to London to live independently, close to their biological mother. The youngest had remained with the carer under difficult circumstances, particularly after the carer's husband died; the lad was also experiencing mental health problems. I was specifically requested by a senior manager to become involved as a sessional worker to the family. My role was to support the carer and to act as a mentor or role model to the client by taking him out on weekend trips to give the foster mother some respite. My involvement with this family in general, and the teenager in particular, made a big difference. In the absence of his biological parents, he came to see me in those roles.

I also made contact with his brothers, who not only appreciated my involvement but began to take an active role in his welfare. My intervention with this family culminated in the lad's move to London to be reunited with his family. I was credited by social services for the work, which also laid my foundation as a Black African social worker in this area. I enjoyed the work and was proud to be able to make a difference. This particular intervention and the successful outcome laid the foundation for my involvement years later as mentor to Black students at the university.

As the leader of the outreach team, I took account of the

mistakes and misguided practices of earlier decades and the difficult experience local authorities had in recruiting Black carers for Afro-Caribbean children. At the time, my white social work colleagues, who were assessing foster carers, had no knowledge or awareness of Black families or cultures and therefore, in their assessment of Afro-Caribbean families, they tended to apply standard Eurocentric criteria in determining 'good enough' parental skills. I incorporated this cultural awareness into our assessment of all our prospective carers.

Doing so didn't come without reaction and criticisms. A common view held by local authorities and foster carers was that all children had the same needs and therefore should be accorded the same care and treatment. While I appreciate that view was used to ensure that there would be no prejudice against Black children, I felt that it was a misguided view. My own experience both of growing up in England and from the work I had done with African teenagers had led me to conclude that Black children and children from minority ethnic backgrounds needed to have an awareness of identity and to have their specific needs recognised.

Again, drawing on my own experiences, I believed that in addition to dietary and health needs, Black children also needed to have a sense of their history and to be able to celebrate their origins. Other than sports, the limited positive role models available to Black children in public life and the media tended to be the negative ones they saw on television. With the responsibility I had, I firmly believed that foster carers needed to recognise this challenge and help the Black children in their care to deal with such issues and stereotypes. Traditional views had to be challenged. For instance, having to say to children that you don't notice race or skin colour and that 'sticks and stones will break my bones but words cannot hurt you'. Such views may be expressed with good intentions but I feel they are misguided because, from my experience of working with Black children and teenagers, what they need is someone to help them celebrate their identity.

As an outreach team leader, I certainly did not believe that only Black families could meet the needs of Black children. I was clear to my team that if we recruited Black foster carers, they might support children from any ethnic background. This proved successful and we were able to recruit a few carers from minority ethnic backgrounds who offered sheltered accommodation to white children, until we were challenged by the racist response of some white families whose children had been placed with an Asian carer. What really astonished me was when the white parents indicated to me that they did not want their children placed with a 'curry eating' family. Ironically, these children had been placed in the care of the local authority because of physical abuse within the family.

In addition to our awareness training and the supportive role of our sessional workers we were able to achieve our objectives: helping Black children, particularly those placed with white families including in predominantly white neighbourhoods to develop mechanisms for coping with racism. As the team entered its second year, we were acknowledged in social services as a valuable resource; in particular, I was given credit and recognition for my role in leading the team.

The next phase I had to steer through involved the gradual transferring of the foster carers we had recruited and supported to the department fostering team, under the condition that my team would continue to facilitate monthly carer's support group meetings for all carers. I continued to retain control and accountability for the pool of sessional workers which other teams could access via means of a referral to outreach.

Initially set-up as a two-year specialist project, the team ran successfully for over a year longer than planned. During that time, numerous changes had either taken place or were being planned. William had retired and the post had been filled. The overall management and coordination of the three separate services (residential, court and outreach) within the centre was being reviewed with the view to having a community services manager on-site and managerially responsible for the coordination of the three areas.

When the community services manager's post was advertised, the court officer and I submitted applications. We were both shortlisted and interviewed together with a number of other internal and external candidates. The interview was rigorous, and, consistent with the times, subjective in the sense that candidates were not necessarily asked the same questions. I was rather disappointed that the appointment went to an external candidate who, by coincidence, had also completed her social work training in my year and group.

My memories of that interview relate more to the discussion that occurred after it between the court officer and myself. When I went to his office to commiserate with him, his prejudice was clearly revealed when he remarked, 'Well, I didn't expect you to get it.' I was shocked by his remark but remained determined to crack the glass ceiling at all cost.

It was during the final year of the outreach team when the Central Council for Education and Training in Social Work (CCETSW) decided to amalgamate and standardise the social work qualification across both field and residential services. Since the residential qualification (CSS) had not included in-depth child protection work, holders of the CSS were required to do a six-month part-time top-up postgraduate course in child protection.

The organisational process and timeline for phasing out the outreach team was less than satisfactory and did not do justice to the individuals in the team who had contributed to the success of the project. We were more or less left on our own to explore career and job alternatives. In my case, I began to consider various choices. After two failed attempts at middle-managerial positions and almost eight years of my career in a residential setting, I felt that perhaps it was time to move in a different direction, into the wider community.

As luck would have it, I was informally approached by one of the community services managers and asked to consider a move to her children and families' social work team. I didn't need much persuading. I had almost completed my child protection training, and this was the ideal opportunity to put it to practice. I was also flattered that I had been headhunted by the manager of a department. I accepted her suggestion to visit the team and glean some insight into the work and philosophy of the team. Following the visit, I formalised my request for a transfer into the children and families team.

Reflecting on the start of my career as residential group leader and the three years spent as group leader and manager for the specialist outreach project, I felt it was a positive and enlightening experience. First and foremost, I enjoyed working with residential staff and made many lifelong friends. I had some good managers whose advice and guidance I appreciated and who allowed me to grow and develop my skills as a practitioner. However, it was time to move on and diversify. More than anything, I gained valuable experience in managing and prioritising resources and working with the public. I also learned a lot about the organisational culture and the politics that are played within the organisation and it would be disingenuous to pretend I did not play some of the politics myself.

I owed a lot to the outreach project which, without a doubt, brought me to prominence within the organisation and boosted my profile and recognition as a competent Black professional. I recall another Black social worker being employed at that time and his planned induction had included a meeting with me. Not having had a role model when I joined the organisation, I was pleased that I could provide that for other Black professionals. It also made me all the more determined to put more cracks in the glass ceiling.

I was under no illusion of what that might mean and how it could be achieved, but I had sheer determination and grit on my side.

PART 3

Changing Direction

CHAPTER 9

Social work in the community

THE BEGINNING OF JULY 1989 BROUGHT A NEW START and a different challenge. Supported by my family, I finally made my big move, eight years after joining the local authority, into the community as a field social worker within a children and family patch team. The team was one of five patches covering Hastings and St Leonards. It had been acknowledged that I was bringing to the team my experience of working directly with children and my specialist knowledge of local resources, including fostering and sheltered accommodation for young people. Although the transfer brought financial rewards and benefits, it meant losing my status as a group leader and also starting in a new team with different responsibilities and accountabilities in terms of child protection procedures and legislations.

The post of team manager or leader was vacant when I arrived and those duties were being performed by the assistant. However, the day-to-day running of the team and the social work team was the responsibility of the community services manager, the person who had encouraged me to apply for my new post as field social worker. There was also a senior practitioner and a group of qualified field social workers and assistant social workers.

After years of being responsible for the professional work of others, I was looking forward to the freedom of being supervised by another person with whom 'the buck stopped'. In all honesty, I had mixed feelings about the loss of the status that I had previously enjoyed with the outreach team. I was also aware that I would be the only, and perhaps first, Black social worker in the team.

On the Monday morning of my arrival, I was warmly welcomed by the acting team manager, Geoff, who met me in his office. Instead of the customary chat about my induction and how to familiarise myself with the team and our patch, he asked if I recognised the name of a sixteen-year-old lad whose first name was John. I did, from my time as group leader at Old Roar. I anticipated the direction in which the conversation was heading. John had been arrested during the night and was being detained at the local police station pending a magistrate's court hearing later that morning. So instead of the anticipated induction, I found myself being allocated my first case and asked to attend court. If this had taken me by surprise, for my client it was even more so; he was also slightly amused when I arrived at the police station to inform him that I was his social worker.

During the court proceedings, I was asked to summarise my department's immediate plans for this lad were he to be released that day. Thanks to my previous position and contacts, I confidently informed the court that he would be accommodated with one of our approved carers. Based on this assurance, after a quick phone call to the carer, the lad was remanded on bail to the local authority. Such was my baptism by fire into the community team!

While there were similarities between residential and field social work, there were also significant differences. The nature of the work required learning and adopting new intervention skills and an adherence to a more rigid legal framework. The culture of the community team differed with the long shifts and unsociable hours of residential care replaced by independent case work.

One of the first things I learned related to our supervisor, Mary Williams, the community services manager (CSM), and her mood swings. I felt that social workers within the team had different views of her: some saw her as having favourites, while others believed that she could be temperamental. I fell into the latter category. Having joined the team at her invitation and, at a time when I was looking for a break and a change of direction, generally I found her supportive and helpful, albeit rather too motherly at times. She suffered badly from arthritis and one could guess the intensity of her pain according to her behaviour. She either said hello or pretended you did not exist. On the plus side, her views and knowledge of diversity and race issues and related legislations were up-to-date and better than I had anticipated. I attributed this to the fact that she had moved to Hastings, having previously worked in London and the surrounding areas, where diversity and multiculturalism were more prevalent.

As social workers we had heavy caseloads, including child protection cases, and on any given day it was not unusual to leave the office in the morning for community visits only to return long after closing hours. Fortunately, at that time, we did not have the additional problems of dealing with bureaucracy and paperwork which later were to become a feature of social work. To her credit, Mary was one of those managers who remained in the office until all the workers had either returned or updated her on their personal safety. I had the impression that she was hard working while also endeavouring to establish herself as a female professional in what was a predominantly white male culture. As a Black male, I identified and empathised with her issues; however, I was even more determined to break through the invisible barriers, the glass ceiling.

Within a few weeks of joining the team the local authority was faced with an unprecedented child protection investigation which attracted both national and local media attention. There had been allegations of inappropriate sexual behaviour by the headmaster of a private co-educational school. It was both a day and boarding school and the majority of the pupils were from Africa and Asia. As the school was in my team's patch, the primary responsibility for mobilising and co-ordinating the appropriate agencies to deal with the case rested with us. The immediate action taken by the local authority following the arrest of the headmaster was to take over the running of the school. We set about contacting the parents in order to inform them about the allegations and the procedures which had been put in place. We interviewed some of the male boarders and notified some of the relevant embassies regarding our actions and intervention, updating them on the welfare of the children.

Many of the teaching staff were unhappy with our intervention and investigation. Fortunately, the local authority had a family centre in the vicinity which became the hub for our investigation. A team of social workers, including myself, were put together to supervise and work with the boarders. My ethnicity, colour and experience of boarding school, coupled with my residential social work experiences became very helpful to the local authority and to the boarders, especially those from West Africa, and it proved useful in my communications with their parents.

It was no surprise to me, understanding their culture, that the parents with whom I spoke were more concerned with the disruption in their children's education and less interested in the child protection issues. Child sexual abuse and investigation were seen as Western matters. I explained to my colleagues the cultural issues we were confronting and that it was misguided to assess some of the parents as being unconcerned. They were simply more concerned with their children's academic studies in which they had invested substantially, just as my parents had done for me. The value of an English education was that it would help ensure their future success. Despite the circumstances, it was satisfying being able to communicate properly with the students and their parents and being able to explain to the families by telephone, the process and progression of the investigation. Most of the West African students seemed proud to see a social worker from that region and they were happy to chat with me about life in England and my own experiences of the British education system.

This investigation lasted for three weeks. The initial allegations were substantiated and the school was closed down. To add to the trauma experienced by those students who had cooperated with the investigation was the fact that the headmaster committed suicide, anticipating the investigation's outcome. The next dilemma faced by the local authority was whether or not to place all the pupils involved on the local authority at risk register. We did not have the resources to monitor them all. We also had to consider the necessity and effectiveness of doing so as the students were about to travel home, most abroad to their families. Consequently, we didn't pursue that course of action.

Working on the investigation with a team of other professionals, including the police, was a valuable experience for me. After the closure of the school, I returned to my regular work and my office, which I shared with three colleagues, one being the wife of the assistant director. Several weeks after my return, she approached me early one morning and asked how I had enjoyed the previous evening's buffet dinner. She seemed most surprised when I responded by asking her which dinner and she responded 'the thank you dinner'. The local authority, in appreciation of the work done by the team assigned to the school, had decided to invite all the professionals involved to dinner. I had not received an invitation.

When I decided to find out why I had not been included, I was told that it had been an oversight by the administrative assistant. I received a formal apology from the assistant director. Yet I found it incredible that the only Black social work professional involved in the investigation of a private school with predominantly Black pupils was the only member of the team who was not invited, ostensibly because of an administrative error. It was difficult to share my feelings with anyone else on the team though.

With the investigation completed, I focused my energy on integrating and getting to know my new team. It was a good learning curve and went more smoothly than I had anticipated. I was aware of my strengths, limitations and experiences; even so, there were a lot of experienced practitioners within the team who offered guidance and support to me. It seemed like a great team, even taking into account the different personalities and viewpoints. One of the elephants in the room remained any discussion of race – until, that is, the introduction of a new legislation, The Children's Act, 1989.

The Act listed factors which had to be taken into account by local authorities in any decisions or assessments in respect of the welfare of children. It placed a duty on us to give due consideration to the child's religion, race, culture and language.

Although the department had organised formal training sessions across the county, Mary, CSM, and her line manager, Sally, felt that a team-building and training day was appropriate to help us familiarise ourselves and discuss the implications of the new Act and our statutory duties and responsibilities within the legislation. In their preparation for the away day, the two managers decided to incorporate race awareness issues into the agenda. We frontline workers were never consulted or asked for suggestions or input during the planning of the event. Some simply saw it as a day away from the office and child protection duties.

The morning sessions on the day itself were mainly devoted to discussions around organisational and policy issues and on how effective we felt communication was within the team and the organisation. Those sessions did have some of the ingredients of team building and cohesion and we were feeling relaxed and stress-free at lunch. The later sessions were going to focus on practice issues and the action plan for implementing the new act, with a particular focus on race, culture and ethnicity. I felt positive about being able to make a valuable contribution to those discussions.

The afternoon began with a recap and an overview of the morning session and what had been achieved. This was followed by a request to us to form small groups for the next task. We were instructed to discuss and list 'commonly held stereotypes of Black people'. Instantly I felt uncomfortable and as the only Black person in the room, self-consciously visible. The thought running through my mind was whether in preparing this exercise the facilitators had considered that they would be asking me to contribute to a list of stereotypes about my race. I sat in my small group feeling exposed, vulnerable and distressed about the task, none of which I could share with my colleagues because they had no understanding or awareness of Black issues. Prior to that training session race awareness and diversity training had not been introduced and this new legislation was meant to start that awareness. To say that I felt humiliated was an understatement.

While my colleagues were busy with the assigned task, I sat wondering how the facilitators would draw the exercise to a conclusion, how they would proceed in their analysis of the stereotypes and particularly how that information would inform or benefit good social work practice and intervention with Black service users. My colleagues seemed to me to lack any consideration of how I might be feeling in that moment.

To my astonishment my presence did not seem to inhibit the discussions around me and although I was in a group, I began to listen more to the conversations around me: the phenomenon described as the 'cocktail party syndrome'. Eventually, we were called to a plenary and the two managers proceeded to collect the A1 feedback sheets from the groups which were carefully placed on the wall. I felt incredibly uncomfortable as I glanced at the charts, but the worst was yet to come.

Having attached the sheets to the wall, the managers, with markers in their hands, proceeded to work through the lists, ticking off the stereotypes while making comments like: 'This one is not true' or 'Obviously, this is not true.' I couldn't help noticing the large number of unticked stereotypes which they seemed unable to fit into either of their categories. The atmosphere in the room changed and there was a pin-drop silence. I sat wondering whether my colleagues would challenge or comment on the analysis that had resulted from their contributions. There was no such response and sensing the uncomfortable silence in the room, the facilitators tried to shift the focus by moving to a different item on the agenda.

I was feeling angry and visibly isolated in the group. However, it was at this point that I felt I needed to make my feelings known and to let the managers and my colleagues know how the exercise had left me feeling. I also felt I needed to give the team my honest evaluation of that activity. Ironically in doing so, I became particularly mindful of trying not to come across as aggressive, given that aggression had been one of the un-ticked stereotypes on most of the flipcharts.

The exercise took my mind back to my freshman year as a psychology student at Calvin college when we had to review the 1933 research study by D. Katz and K. Braly on racial stereotyping. The authors presented 100 university students with a number of characteristics from which to choose and asked the students to select the five characteristics that were most applicable to different groups of people, this despite the fact that very few of the students in the study had come into contact with the different groups. What transpired from the research was that white Americans were attributed the characteristics of 'industrious and intelligent' whereas Black Americans were attributed the characteristics of 'superstitious, lazy and musical'. Japanese were also seen as 'intelligent and industrious'.

Stereotypes can be negative or positive, and they do not only affect the behaviour of those doing the stereotyping but of those being stereotyped. In the latter, it can create extra demands and lead to impaired performance. I was determined not to allow this to happen to me and to ensure that as a team the negative stereotypes of Black people did not affect the delivery of services to Black service users or those wanting to gain access to the services.

When I arrived home that evening, still angry and dis-appointed, I thought about the day and tried to rationalise about what had happened. As two professionals, nurse and social worker, my wife Karen and I always endeavoured to separate our professional lives from our private lives. We did that by not bringing our work issues and difficulties home with us. Home was for the family. Consequently, I did not share the events of the team day with her.

My colleagues again made me reflect back on my days as a psychology student and the work of the social psychologist Irving Janis, in particular. Janis asserted that a group places a higher value on harmony and the desire to conform than to critically evaluate and analyse a situation. This phenomenon, which he identified as 'groupthink', can also explain how group decisions may differ from the views of the individuals within the group, something I was to observe early the following morning when I arrived at the office.

There were limited office parking spaces, which gave an advantage to arriving early at work. It also gave me freedom to plan my day before the others arrived. Mary was another early arrival that morning. Before going to her office, she stopped by mine to offer an apology. She said that it was only later at home when she thought about the day that she had come to realise the true significance of the activity and how I must have felt as the only Black person in the room.

I did not question the apology that followed, which came across as genuine. Practically every team member then made their way to my office that morning to also apologise. After a few days, the team appeared to have moved on from that unfortunate event, but for me, the healing process lasted much longer. The event was a learning curve for me in terms of my experiences and strategies for coping with racism and racial stereotypes. One of the hard lessons though was that while some colleagues might be empathic and supportive to me on an individual level, they were reluctant to be so publicly, maybe for fear of rocking their career boat.

One positive outcome for me was that team day enhanced my visibility as a Black social worker and promoted my desire and interest in social work training so that I might make a difference. What I had endured that day brought to the fore the subject of race. It highlighted many of the issues Black professionals working in a predominantly white workforce were encountering on a regular basis, including whether or not to share their feelings and experiences of prejudice and racism with their white supervisors and the fear that by doing that, it might make things even worse.

There was a time when the negative experiences of Black workers would have been dismissed, as I said in chapter seven, with comments or phrases like 'you've got a chip on your shoulder', 'you're being too sensitive' or, as in my experience, 'you must be used to that by now'. Consequently, Black professionals often had to develop unique coping mechanisms and strategies for dealing with issues of racism and stereotypes while at the same time not allowing those issues to get in the way of their careers. As a result, some Black professionals in predominantly white organisations find themselves working extremely hard, while having to suppress the effects of racism.

The experience of dealing with racism in the workplace was often more than just having to challenge racial stereotypes from colleagues. Returning to the question of 'what it was like for me', the answers became more complex when I moved from residential social work into the community where I had to work with some service users who actually refused to work with or to be allocated a Black social worker. One such case stands out in my memory because of the effect it had on me both psychologically and emotionally.

Mary had agreed to accept the transfer of a child protection case from another area because the children in the family had resettled in our area and it had been allocated to me. The case involved two children who were allegedly sexually abused over a period of time by three of their mother's male friends. One of the alleged abusers was described in the case summary as a Black man. Since no description and identity of the other two men were mentioned in the summary, I assumed that they were white. The father had been granted custody and at the time of the case transfer conference, the children were happily settled in a local school.

In those days, parents were not normally invited to attend case conferences. Instead, following the meeting, the social worker would contact or visit the family to update them on the outcome and decision. This particular meeting was attended by all the professionals and agencies involved with the children's welfare, including the school, the health visitor, police and, of course, social services, represented by my manager, myself and the manager for child protection conferences.

A few days before, I chatted with the social worker who was making the transfer. He told me that the father had a good sense of humour and he thought he and I would get along well. Surprisingly, during the conference neither the chair nor the other professionals remarked on our limited information about two of the alleged abusers in comparison to the considerable details known about the Black man. This crossed my mind, but I felt powerless to raise it during the conference, simply because case conferences at the time were formal and highly structured. They were very hierarchical, and being a new worker in the team I did not have the professional confidence or support.

Afterwards, I wrote to the father to introduce myself and to arrange a home visit to inform him of the case conference's decision. However, two days later the school informally told him about the conference and me, the new social worker. I heard that he went ballistic when told that the family social worker was Black and made it clear to the school that he would not accept that for his children. He further stated that if I went to his house, as had been planned that afternoon, 'he would not be responsible' for his actions.

The school immediately contacted my office, hoping to warn me against the visit, but I had already left to make appointments before the one with this family. I arrived at the house as planned and rang the bell. After several rings, there was no response. This was not unusual: social workers are accustomed to some service users not opening their doors to us. As I stood outside the house, there were clear indications that there were people inside; I could hear the voices of children. In the end, I decided to go back to the office.

On my return, I was met by my manager, who called me to her office. She proceeded to explain the situation and the message that had been received from the school. I could sense the difficulty she was having in trying to choose appropriate language. Ultimately, she did so and we sat in silence. I was shocked and caught off guard when she asked me if I felt I could continue to attempt to engage with this family or whether the case should be reallocated to another social worker, obviously a white one. She showed no empathy towards me, and the issue of racism remained unspoken. My response in the end was that I needed time to digest and reflect on that afternoon's events before I could make a decision, one based not on my qualifications, experience and skills, but purely on my ethnicity and colour.

We resumed the meeting the following morning, after I had time to think. I came prepared and determined to lead the discussion and not be driven by the organisational agenda. I informed her that I felt there was an urgent need for some ongoing social work intervention with the family and that the welfare of the two children was of paramount importance. On that basis, I said while I was not happy, I accepted that the case should be reallocated to another white colleague. It was a stressful meeting. I was angry that I had little option other than to make that decision and it was difficult to express how I felt, knowing that my choices were limited and that I was not in an environment where I could express my feelings and anticipate support and understanding. I often wondered if the colleague to whom the case was reallocated ever thought about the circumstances in which she came to it. The incident was never discussed, however.

Almost thirty years later, there are those who would optimistically conclude that things have improved. Granted, there have been changes in policies and in social work training and education. In East Sussex, however, where the Black and minority ethnic population is less than eight percent of the total, those numbers are still not reflected in the workforce of the local authority. Looking at the current political and social climate and the 'Black lives matter' movement, my observation and assessment is that changes over the years have not been significant.

Engagement photo of me and Karen in 1970

Family gatherings and events have always been treasured.
Here I am sharing my joy with my four grandchildren, Theo,
Solomon, Jacob and Olivia.

With Karen and Michelle on Michael's 18th birthday.

Graduation from London University.

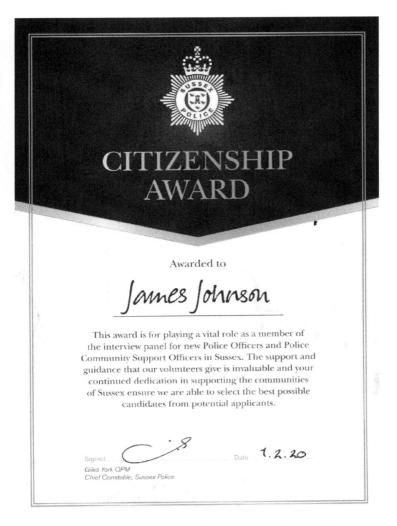

CITIZENSHIP AWARD

Awarded to

James Johnson

This award is for playing a vital role as a member of the interview panel for new Police Officers and Police Community Support Officers in Sussex. The support and guidance that our volunteers give is invaluable and your continued dedication in supporting the communities of Sussex ensure we are able to select the best possible candidates from potential applicants.

Signed .... Date 1.2.20

Giles York QPM
Chief Constable, Sussex Police

Citizenship ceremony award from Sussex police in 2020.

CHAPTER 10

Making a difference: addiction and HIV/AIDS

THE STATUTORY DUTY OF THE TEAM was to work directly with children and families, usually under the umbrella of safeguarding children and preventative social work which involved an assessment of external factors in the community which can lead to or exacerbate problems within families. To remedy this, we were encouraged by our community services manager to build up specialist knowledge and interest and to forge closer liaisons with community groups and schools within our catchment area. Each social worker was given a school liaison role and responsibility whereby the school could ring for advice and guidance and to alert the social worker about possible concerns. The range of specialist interest and knowledge within the team included welfare rights and benefits, housing issues, alcohol and substance misuse.

While some colleagues opted to specialise in child protection, I did not lean towards it. While I had had some previous negative experiences, I also felt that my career in that arena would not progress or advance, because of the existing glass ceiling. Instead, I became interested in social issues such as substance misuse, housing and links with marginalised groups in the community. In order to develop this specialist knowledge, I was encouraged to attend external training courses on drugs and alcohol and to form links with the relevant agencies in the area.

Every ten days, I was rostered to do social work duties, which meant being available to respond to any situation or visitors coming in to see a social worker. As a duty social worker, I initially had difficulties connecting or engaging with clients who came into the office under the influence of alcohol. I attributed this to my ignorance, and to prejudices and stereotypes. Working as a duty social worker forced me to engage with and to try to develop an understanding of clients who had been labelled alcoholics by society. Perhaps ironically, our office was located next door to a pub which was frequented by service users, some of whom would wander into the office after afternoon closing for no reason other than to hurl abuse at the duty social worker.

One such visitor was the father of John, the lad I referred to earlier. He would come to the office duty desk following a lunchtime drinking session to question whoever was on duty about his son and the reasons why social services had placed him in care. He would proceed to inform us that his son was now drinking and sleeping on the street, that John had turned out worse than himself. It was very difficult to deal with this man and the many others in an intoxicated condition. I began to question my own prejudices in order to understand the world of people with alcohol dependency and the effect of their dependency on their families and the wider community.

It was as a result of my self-analysis that I decided to pursue and add substance misuse to my specialist interests. I was given the opportunity to attend many training courses and seminars on drugs and alcohol misuse. I also made contact and links with all the specialist alcohol and drugs services in the area. In a relatively short-time, I had acquired a good knowledge of the law and an understanding of the needs of people with that dependency.

My experience and liaison with specialist substance misuse services in the community made me aware that this group of clients was marginalised, stigmatised and frequently denied access to many statutory and supportive services. As a social worker, I was determined to make a difference, either directly through my engagement or indirectly through advocacy and empowerment. In my caseload, there were many families affected by alcohol dependence; however, there was one which stands out in my memory, where I felt I made a significant difference.

Working with the Mason family not only changed my attitude, it also enhanced my knowledge and understanding of addiction and the damaging effect it has on families. Once upon a time, in common with the public and the police, I would have labelled Miss Mason, the mother, a bad parent. However, taking a professional stance, I could see that she was more inadequate than bad. She wanted to change her dependent behaviour and the rituals associated with that behaviour, but she lacked the motivation and support to change and the agencies to which she was referred put the onus for change back on her.

I was able to connect, engage and build up a positive relationship with the family even when my intervention on two occasions necessitated the removal of the children from home, their placement in temporary care and their names on the child protection 'at risk' register. Because of the mother's inability to keep appointments, I often had to meet the children at their school at the end of the day to walk them home where they would frequently be met by the mother and her regular group of drinking friends. By networking with other professionals like her doctor and specialist counselling services and advocating with welfare and other statutory services, I gained the trust of the family and began to see a change in both her behaviour and parenting.

Through my intervention with this family, I became familiar with both the social model and medical model of alcoholism. Drugs and alcohol misuse and addiction are issues which have both medical and social consequences;

they therefore require a holistic multi-agency approach. In the mother's case, it was not about the quantity of alcohol she drank daily but more about her relationship with the alcohol and with the friends with whom she associated. Although my knowledge of drugs and substance misuse was limited, it was nevertheless a useful resource and a valuable asset to the team which enabled us to identify the gaps and how to respond to clients with similar problems. I also felt that the discrimination this mother faced because of her chosen lifestyle was in some ways similar to my own experiences of discrimination and isolation, encountered purely on the basis of the colour of my skin.

In the 1980s, another area of specialist interest emerged as a result of the HIV (human immunodeficiency virus) crisis. A hysterical media response brought stigma and discrimination towards those affected by HIV. This was linked to its association with premature death, homosexuality and Black people. Haitians and Black Africans were blamed. The negative responses to sufferers echoed those faced by my clients with alcohol and drug dependency.

When news of HIV reached England, I was the group leader at the children's centre. I clearly remember the principal bringing up the subject of AIDS (acquired immunodeficiency virus) at a staff meeting. He asked the team for a show of hands to indicate which of us, if any, as residential workers would be willing to work with someone who had AIDS. With his limited knowledge of the epidemic, he connected the new epidemic to the African continent. As an African, and with family living in Africa, I naturally became interested in knowing more about the disease. I also wondered if and how my family in Africa might be affected.

When I moved into the community team as a children and families social worker, I became more interested in HIV/AIDS and incorporated it into my development portfolio. Families were affected by HIV in several ways, I found. My casework involved parents with HIV whose children required services as they became sick and died. It involved children with HIV, where the families needed help and social support. I also had cases where the children and their mothers were affected and that necessitated long-term intervention and planning. My interest in HIV was also triggered by a friend who, knowing that I was a social worker, confided in me that her son had been tested positive for the 'AIDS virus'. Witnessing first-hand the family's experience, I helped them to deal with practical issues as well as matters relating to confidentiality and disclosure.

I attended numerous seminars and training events about HIV in order to advance my specialist knowledge and expertise and also to act as the resource person within the team, particularly when a number of HIV cases were being reported in our area. We had a case of a mother who had become infected with the virus following a blood transfusion during the birth of her son. He also tested positive months later. At that stage of social services involvement a few years later, the mother had become very ill and there were some medical concerns about the health of her son, who had just started school.

HIV/AIDS was perhaps the first epidemic that was experienced by the majority of the population through the media of newspapers and television. Media reporting identified HIV/AIDS with homosexuality, provoking fear of contagion, blame and prejudice. The government's response was in the form of a 'Don't Die of Ignorance' leaflet posted to every household to educate the public about the epidemic along with TV and billboard adverts. Unlike other medical conditions HIV/AIDS was associated with two powerful stigmata: contracting an infectious disease that could lead to death and homophobia, a negative value judgement about homosexuals and homosexual behaviour. Despite the identification of other infected groups and heterosexuals, the negative public perception and association of the disease with alternative lifestyles was reinforced by the media.

Local authorities throughout the country took on board the message. With a ring-fenced budget and the AIDS support grant from central government, my local authority employed its first specialist HIV/AIDS social worker. The local authority also inaugurated a one-day basic awareness training programme with the primary aim and objective of providing all its staff with basic, factual, up-to-date information on the virus to enable them to work with those infected as well as affected by the virus. A pool of dedicated in-house staff from across the organisation were selected and trained to facilitate this monthly training and to work closely with the specialist worker. I was nominated to the pool of trainers.

Concurrently with this development, the Department of

Health issued guidelines for local authorities which made specific reference to training and further recommended that all staff involved in working with or supervising children and their managers should receive basic training in respect of children with HIV/AIDS in order to promote awareness of the virus among service providers.

At the time, I strongly advocated for and stressed the need for social workers to be involved in working with people infected with and affected by HIV. I could see that social work intervention presented us with significant moral and ethical dilemmas as well as challenges to our traditional client/worker relationship and its boundaries. I could see that intervention and direct social work with HIV service users also presented many counter-transference issues which all professionals, including social workers needed to address. Some of these included the fear of contagion, the terminal illness and death of people who were often of similar ages, professional helplessness and inadequacy and, at times, over-identification with service users and their problems. From my social work perspective, the HIV epidemic highlighted the need for effective and sensitive supervision and anti-discriminatory practices which are fundamental principles underlying social work training and practice.

While there were similarities between HIV and substance misusers, in that both groups were stigmatised and marginalised by the public and experienced difficulties accessing services, I soon realised that there were also significant differences and that those differences were in my legal framework and mandate for our intervention and, as a social worker, my statutory duties and responsibilities. As a social worker, while I knew that I had a duty to my clients, I also recognised that I had a duty to society and to uphold the law. The key principle of the Misuse of Drugs Act is to prevent the unauthorised use of substances that are capable of having harmful effects and that it is an offence to possess, supply or produce. It was important that I was cognisant of this legislation and had a clear understanding of my responsibilities and duties under the law, particularly when visiting a client or service user on premises where there might be proscribed drugs and the possibility of a police raid. It could be challenging to build a meaningful and trusting relationship with some clients aware of a social worker's statutory and legal responsibilities.

Much as I enjoyed the challenges and experiences of working in a children and families team, the high volume of cases and the statutory responsibilities did not always allow me to build and maintain the quality of professional interaction necessary to effect positive changes and desired outcomes.

When I recall my supervision in children and families services, it could be described as little more than a 'tick box' exercise. It seemed the manager wanted to cover her back by putting on record that she had discussed and given advice about a case. This was due to the statutory nature of the work. To my disappointment, those sessions were rarely about my development as a practitioner and after two years, I came to the conclusion that I needed to pursue a different career path to avoid becoming burned out by the stresses of child protection work. I needed a change from trying to engage with service users who really did not want my intervention but were forced to accept it because of the powers of the local authority.

Although there were a number of HIV/AIDS cases in our local authority area, Brighton, the adjacent authority, some forty miles away, had one of the highest numbers of HIV/AIDS cases outside of London. The incumbent specialist HIV social worker was offered a higher specialist managerial position with that authority, leaving a vacancy. When the vacant post was advertised, I spoke with my manager, who had already anticipated that I would be interested. My discussion with her centred on the fact that the post was part-time and the worker would be based in the hospital social work team. She was understanding and keen to help, suggesting that I could combine the part-time specialist post, if offered, with a part-time post in her team.

This would mean holding two part-time posts across both children and adult services. Although this type of arrangement had never happened before, it was an attractive proposition, so I applied for the Brighton-based specialist worker's post.

A week before the interview, however, I suddenly received the distressing news from Liberia that my mother had died. My focus shifted to making plans for my travel back for the funeral and having to leave Karen and the kids at home for a week. When I attended the interview a few days before my departure for Africa, I did not share that information, because I did not want my sad news to deflect from the interview.

Only after I was informed that I had been successful and offered the position did I make public my mother's death and subsequent trip to Liberia.

The outcome of my new appointment meant that I would be accountable to two community services managers, one in adult services and the other in children's services. Details of my working days and schedule were worked out between the two managers following my return from Liberia. I would be spending two and a half days a week in the hospital setting and another two and a half days in the patch team in St Leonards. Because of the proximity of the two working locations, there was some room for flexibility in the arrangement.

Following my return from Liberia, I had a two-week handover period with Andy, whose job I was taking over, before his departure. During this induction, I had the opportunity to visit many of the clients with him. I soon realised that there was a difference between textbook knowledge of HIV and the reality. Few of the clients I met matched the images portrayed in the media. I was forced to confront my own unfounded fear of contagion, even though I knew about HIV transmission. Although my reaction was short-lived, it enabled me to understand the general public's fears.

I quickly realised that holding two totally different part-time jobs was a flawed and unsustainable arrangement. It was tantamount to working two full-time jobs. While I regarded working across services as a balancing act, it was impossible to meet all of its challenges: my children and families caseload was reduced, but I frequently had to return to children services because this took priority over my HIV work. I found myself in the position of having to make another decision about where I felt I was best suited and could make the most valuable contributions to service users. At the time there was a perceived difference in status and recognition between social workers in children services and those in adult services. It was often expressed in derogatory terms that that one did not need a professional qualification to work in adult services. This persisting negative view was articulated by our area manager when we met at a Christmas social event. He approached me and said that he had been made to understand that I was leaving children services and going into adult services and when I confirmed this was indeed the case, he retorted 'what a waste of a career'. I was determined to prove him wrong.

The community services manager in the hospital team had given me a permanent job offer which combined part-time generic hospital social work with part-time specialist HIV social worker under one manager. As a hospital social worker, I was assigned to cover and provide social work input and assessment on the orthopaedic ward at the hospital.

With my HIV clients, I was working mostly with young people, while on the orthopaedic ward I was dealing mostly with the elderly. It was a good mix of a service user group. Unlike the social work model of intervention to which I had been trained, in the hospital setting and with medical professionals I was working with a medical model in terms of diagnosis and treatment. The structure and culture in the medical team was hierarchical. This was very evident during the weekly ward meetings in which the doctors were addressed by their titles and it seemed important not to confuse the title of 'Mr' with that of 'Dr'. The female nurses were referred to as 'girls' by the doctors. Since the doctors addressed me by my first name, I reciprocated by doing the same to them. I also had to become acquainted with medical language and jargon during these meetings. The social work profession has its own jargons, and I regarded this as a learning experience.

Within the hospital setting, particularly on the orthopaedic ward to which I was assigned, I was surprised to see the large number of Afro-Caribbean nurses. From the many conversations I had with them on the ward what they all seemed to have in common was that none of them had risen above staff nurse status. I began to wonder if they too were dealing with similar career barriers and were constrained by a glass ceiling. It also dawned on me that I was the only Black social worker in the hospital and I had been assigned to this ward. Was that on purpose?

Because these Afro-Caribbean nurses did not receive the same level of supervision and support from their line manager as I did from mine, they often approached me to share their stories and experiences of working on the ward. These included being aware that some of the patients' relatives had openly stated that they did not want their loved ones on a ward with 'coloured nurses'. I wasn't sure how the hospital handled comments of this nature. An African nurse told me that she found it peculiar that most of the Black nurses in the hospital seemed to have been assigned to the orthopaedic ward, even though most had stated preferences for other wards. I had a lot of empathy for these nurses and the invisible career barriers they faced purely on the basis of their race. Unlike social services these nurses did not seem to have their management support. I was proud to have been a source of support and assurance to these nurses.

Karen, my wife, also allowed me to see how nurses were treated, through her eyes, and we shared an interest in mentoring and personal development. Having made the sacrifice to put her career on hold since our forced return from Liberia, she now, with the support of our family, decided to resume her career, now that I was settled in my own with the local authority. In 1987, when Michelle was seven and Michael eleven, Karen began a part-time job as an auxiliary in a nursing home in Hastings, and while there became interested in a nursing career. Five years later, in 1992, she enrolled as a student at the University of Brighton. During the period of her studies she did her placement at the Conquest hospital in Hastings, where I was also based at the time. Following the completion of her studies three years later, she received her RGN (Registered General Nurse) degree and worked as staff nurse for five years on a medical ward at the Conquest. She resigned to return to the nursing home as sister nurse. She was given the opportunity at the nursing home to advance her education in the direction of training and mentoring for the nursing home staff and nursing students on placement at the nursing home. We both shared common interests in staff development, mentoring and training. In those days of limited technology where there were no power points, I had a potable overhead projector with acetates at home. These proved valuable to us in planning and rehearsing our respective presentations. Although our target groups were different, nurses and social workers, at time we discovered that there were similarities and common threads and themes running through our presentations. Karen remained at the nursing home until 2008, when she took early retirement to assist in proving care for our grandchildren. Her insights were, and remain, invaluable to me.

PART 4

CARVING OUT MY NICHE

CHAPTER 11

Finding visibility: HIV/AIDS and the local authorities

SPEAKING ON BLACK IDENTITY AND VISIBILITY, Nikki Giovanni, the African-American poet, writer, civil rights activist and educator, said: 'You've got to find a way to let people know you are there.' I was aware of the fact that my visibility would not come from child protection social work because it was an area of social work which attracted my white colleagues. My way of achieving that career visibility was through specialism in social work, and advancement in social work training and education.

As a social work practitioner in the hospital team, I gained valuable experience in working with all categories of patients, irrespective of their diagnoses, ages and gender. However, I stood out as a specialist HIV social worker and also through my work partnering with other professionals, including those in the voluntary sector.

In the early 1980s, when news of a new epidemic sweeping across the globe began to spread, several attempts were made by the Western media to trace the origin of the disease back to Africa. The spread of HIV (human immunodeficiency viruses), as it became known, in both Western Europe and North America contrasted sharply with its rise in developing countries, where most transmissions were occurring through heterosexual sexual contact. My client group, in contrast, also included gay and bisexual men and injecting drug users. In the pre-treatment era a diagnosis of HIV signalled the beginning of major medical, emotional and psychological problems for those infected or affected, not to mention the stigma and the negative value judgements prevalent in society in general at the time.

Direct intervention with service users was the primary focus of my social work. This was both a personal and professional challenge. Personal in that I had to assess and reflect on my own attitudes, prejudices and value judgements on issues relating to sex, sexuality and drug misuse. I soon learned that this new client group was atypical. Because of the negative association of HIV and AIDS (acquired immunodeficiency syndrome) with homosexuality, at the time still stigmatised by many, it was an organisational challenge that tested the local authority's anti-discrimination policies and practices.

HIV/AIDS heightened my awareness of one of society's great taboos in Britain: death and dying. Those living with the virus in the early days were predominantly young gay men, although there were also cases of women with the virus. This pattern was reflected in East Sussex, although there were a significant number of women and children with HIV/AIDS. I remember my own fear of HIV when I was introduced to my first clients, an Italian woman and her son. The mother was infected during pregnancy by her partner, an intravenous drug user. She in turn transmitted the virus to her unborn son.

My professional relationship with HIV clients and their families also differed significantly from the usual social worker and client bond. In the former, I shared their emotions, their fears, their grief and sadness, and attended many funerals. While I was always aware of the professional boundaries within these relationships, that did not prevent me from engaging with families, visiting them in their homes and comforting them when appropriate. More than anything, I respected and understood their need for confidentiality.

My specialist role also included a close liaison with specialist HIV doctors, nurses and local voluntary organisations set up in response to the HIV/AIDS crisis. It was a great example of multi-agency partnership working and pulling together to manage resources. Working with a newly identified virus, it was important to maintain my social work focus. However, it was also important for me to know the medical language, terminology and treatment with which the virus had become associated. This was the language with which my clients communicated; for instance, I had to become familiar with the new medications being prescribed and know about the immune system and significance of various laboratory tests. A familiarity with medical language and terminology was a good learning experience. Social work similarly had its own language and terminology with which other professionals and clients had to become familiar.

As a statutory agency, we needed to develop policies and practice guidelines around confidentiality and how to provide specialist services to people living with HIV and to their families and significant others. In 1991, the Department of Health issued guidelines for local authorities in respect of children with HIV/AIDS. It recommended that all staff working with or supervising children should receive basic HIV awareness training.

As the only HIV specialist social worker in East Sussex, I was privileged to have had access to external training courses, conferences and workshops. With that knowledge, I was able to act as advisor to my local authority. I was nominated to work closely with the senior management in writing policies and practice guidelines in respect of both children and adults with HIV. I took a lead role with the training department, planning and delivering basic HIV/AIDS awareness training. I also facilitated the delivery of the training. My medical and nursing colleagues were supportive in contributing to these sessions. Occasionally service users also participated in these sessions to share their experiences of living with the virus. This helped to dismiss some of the common misleading stereotypes that were around about HIV/AIDS.

Facilitating or co-facilitating basic HIV awareness training became my passion because I felt knowledge of the virus would lead to changes in attitudes. Although the aims and goals of the training were to provide staff with basic factual and up-to-date information about HIV/AIDS, it provided a safe forum for participants to challenge their prejudices and the myths and stigma associated with the virus. In addition to promoting and facilitating HIV/AIDS awareness training, in 1998, I began my part-time master's degree course in mental health social work, commuting weekly to the Institute of Psychiatry at Kings College in London.

The concept of Evidence Based Practice (EBP) was an essential feature of social work practice. As the effectiveness of this basic awareness training had never been evaluated by our training department, I decided to do so for my dissertation, researching and scrutinising the effectiveness of it in altering staff attitudes and tolerance towards clients with HIV/AIDS. Although this was an academic study, my research findings and conclusion were of benefit, as it informed the training department that we were moving in the right direction in terms of changing attitudes and prejudices.

I felt really proud that my research work was valued by the organisation. This made me reflect on the words of Nikki Giovanni about visibility, and I realised I had to find my own way of letting people know I was there. That I might be able to influence and drive policy and training with my research study was something that had never been done before and when I achieved it, I felt it was yet another crack in the organisational glass ceiling.

It was standard policy for social workers to receive formal monthly supervision, either with one's line manager or supervisor. As a lone specialist social worker, supervision was essential. I was fortunate to have a supportive manager with a good grasp and understanding of HIV-related issues. He was different from my previous managers in that he did not feel threatened by aspiring and ambitious workers within his team. Instead, he regularly tapped into the strengths and skills of his team, delegating with trust. More than anyone else before, he encouraged and promoted my career in specialist social work.

Two years into my hospital-based specialist role, I was firmly established and was continuing to demonstrate that I was able to work independently and confidently. A minor restructuring of services created the posts of practice managers and senior practitioners, and in 1997 I was promoted to senior practitioner for the hospital team, responsible for the supervision of all the social workers, including my successor, the newly appointed HIV worker. Another Black social worker had joined the team and, as senior practitioner, I was to be her supervisor. This promotion felt like another crack in the glass ceiling, albeit a small one, yet it was a significant turning point in my career and in my aspirations for higher achievement. There was also an increase in the number of qualified Black social workers in the local authority. I began to feel less isolated professionally. As a group, we began to network and were able to share our experiences of racism and provide support for each other.

In my new position, I was given the time and opportunity to broaden my social work education and training. Social work students on placement were supervised by social workers who had achieved the accredited practice teacher's award. In 1993, after successfully completing this course at Sussex University, I began supervising students on placement in the hospital team. Two years later, I qualified as an approved social worker (ASW). This meant I was now able to carry out assessments under the 1983 Mental Health Act and could be included on the area rota for mental health assessment duties. This new specialism gave me the opportunity to work with doctors and psychiatrists independent of social services, something which I enjoyed.

The powers and remit of an ASW were contained within the framework and guidelines of the 1983 Act. I wanted to learn about the causes and treatment of mental illness and the various ways in which it manifests itself. Given my social work background, I was particularly interested in a psychosocial model of mental illness where the causes could be attributed to societal and environmental factors and how trust could be ameliorated through effective social work intervention.

When the opportunity presented itself, I was encouraged by senior management to further my study in the mental health field. I signed up for a two-year, part-time master's degree course in mental health social work at the University of London. This involved travelling one day a week to the Institute of Psychiatry in Camberwell in south-east London. It was difficult having to juggle my senior practitioner role at the hospital with family commitments and weekly travels to the capital, but I felt the end result was worth it. I also combined my degree with studying for the Advanced Award in Social Work, the highest social work qualification. At the time, only a few people had it in East Sussex.

Being part of the hospital team provided me with the opportunity and experience of working with new service user groups and, as a senior practitioner, I enjoyed supervising social workers, in particular the specialist HIV worker. When I joined the local authority, I was told that being in the middle-management structure of the organisation was like the game of musical chairs: managers were frequently moved around through reorganisation or restructuring. I was about to experience a reconfiguration of services.

As a Black practitioner in a predominately white working culture and environment, I was aware that it was not a career level playing field and so I used specialism and education to highlight my visibility – as Nikki Giovanni advises, to let others know I was there. And it worked.

CHAPTER 12

Substance misuse: changing behaviour

THE ORGANISATIONAL RECONFIGURATION IN 1999 INTRODUCED a new tier of managers in the health team, which left me feeling isolated and unsupported as senior practitioner. Reorganisation was a regular occurrence and I had seen and experienced a significant number over the years. This particular one would create the posts of practice managers, as well as service managers. The manager, Mike, who had been instrumental in encouraging me to transfer from the community to the hospital team, was appointed service manager within the health team, with a new brief that included countywide responsibilities for HIV/AIDS and substance misuse services.

Mike was also a good friend. Recognising how unsupported I was in my current position as a senior practitioner in the hospital team, Mike informally approached me with the offer of a countywide senior practitioner's job for HIV/AIDS and substances misuse services. I found the suggestion difficult to resist, not just because of the new challenges it presented, but also because of its countywide remit. In our meeting, Mike elaborated on his vision and plans, which included extending both HIV/AIDS and substance misuse services. He indicated that he needed someone with my experience and expertise on his team to help him achieve this.

From a career perspective, it seemed the right time to return to the community. The prospect of being instrumental in the setting up the infrastructure and building networks with other agencies and organisations across the county was also attractive. The location was an issue though: the job involved moving from a work base in Hastings, where I was living with my family, to a more central location in Seaford, about 34km away, to the east of Brighton. Ultimately, though, with my family's support, this proved a small compromise.

Within a few months I made the transfer to Seaford, initially on secondment. My office was situated above the library in the centre of town. I made the most of my lunchtime walks on the seafront, some two minutes from the office. I particularly enjoyed the early morning and evening drives to and from work, listening to jazz CDs, usually Ella Fitzgerald, Nancy Wilson or Sarah Vaughan, and having a quiet period of reflection. This time gave me the opportunity to unwind. Daily workouts at the gym are also something I have always enjoyed doing to help me destress. Throughout my professional life, I went straight to the gym from work. This not only helped me relax, but also enabled me to leave the tensions of my work behind before going home to be a husband and father.

My immediate task was to structure the new team. In addition, I would have supervisory responsibilities for four specialist substance misuse social workers across East Sussex, as well as the continuing supervision of the HIV/AIDS social workers based in Eastbourne and Hastings.

One of the plans the service manager discussed with me related specifically to our substance misuse services which, at the time, was not attracting female service users. Women and women with children had historically been discriminated against, denied access to services and to drug treatment and alcoholic facilities because of their perceived childcare respon- sibilities. My previous experience in children and families services had given me insight into some of the existing issues.

Compared to the demographic profile of people with HIV, I found that the characteristics of service users with drug or alcohol dependency were significantly different and presented challenges which required very different responses. For instance, service users with HIV were predominantly younger white males. In contrast, a significant number of our clients dependent on alcohol and drugs presented with a dual diagnosis, mental health and substance dependency. Working with this service user group enabled me to observe the harmful effect and impact of alcohol and drugs on the individual, family and wider community, problems that were often accentuated when children were affected.

In the early and mid-1990s, the availability and range of treatment programmes for alcohol and drug dependencies fell into two broad categories: community or residential rehabilitation. In the case of residential rehabilitation, in order to be eligible, clients had to spend several days in hospital on a detoxification treatment programme immediately prior to commencing the residential programme. Having an awareness of the high cost of doing this, my first mission was to visit a number of residential establishments in Sussex and the neighbouring counties to gain insight into what exactly was being provided.

One treatment programme in particular attracted my attention and concern: the 12-step programme pioneered by Alcoholics Anonymous (AA), also referred to as the Minnesota model for addiction. The progressive steps in the programme began with clients having to admit and acknowledge their powerlessness over alcohol and that life has become unmanageable. Others included the belief that a power greater than themselves could restore sanity and that they must make a decision to turn over their lives to the care of God. Growing up in Liberia in a religious household and experiencing the impact of an adherence to certain religious beliefs and practices, I felt uneasy about strict adherence to this treatment model, especially when I had witnessed clients entering the programme with one problem, addiction, and emerging after a period of treatment with a new one, in my eyes, religion.

Some rehabilitation centres combined the 12 steps with cognitive behaviour therapy (CBT) in their programmes, focusing more on thoughts and feelings. The basic principle underlying CBT is to encourage clients to examine and question their recurring thoughts about alcohol and drugs. Aaron T. Beck, the American psychiatrist, regarded as the father of cognitive therapy and CBT, pioneered CBT in the 1960s. Beck believed that thoughts, feelings and behaviour were linked together. I became familiar with CBT in 1999, while studying for my Masters' degree in mental health social work at the Institute of Psychiatry in London. I passionately believe in CBT as a therapeutic tool for empowering service users to examine their underlying beliefs and feelings, particularly with addiction. However, I was also aware that in this area of social work, the 'one size fits all' approach did not always work and that CBT did not work for everyone with an addiction. I felt it important to treat service users as individuals and always have done so.

Evaluating the various models as a social worker, the one which resonated most with me and which I introduced into the new team assessment process was the 'cycle of change' model, pioneered by psychologists James Prochaska and Carlo DiClementa. They described change as entailing five stages, all involving alterations in attitude and behaviour in order to progress. The stages are pre-contemplation, contemplation, action, maintenance and relapse. I was attracted to this model because, unlike the others, it depicts change as a cycle as supposed to an all-or-nothing step. It also has relapse built into it and therefore, unlike the 12-step model, prevents clients from seeing themselves as failures.

Empowering clients with the tools to change their addictive behaviour was the primary objective and focus of my intervention and subsequent collaboration with other agencies in the health, probation and the voluntary sectors. One of my primary responsibilities was the assessments of suitability of clients for residential rehabilitation and to monitor and review their treatment programme and progress during the placement. Between the agencies, we agreed a standard assessment form which included a forensic history. This involved identifying with clients their weekly expenditure on drugs and alcohol, after which the next step was to compare that amount with their income, generally state benefits. Commonly, clients were spending over a hundred pounds a day on drugs when their income was far less than that in a week. The conclusion often drawn from my assessment was that clients had to resort to crime to fund their dependencies. This information was difficult, raising the ethical issues of how I balanced my social work duty to client confidentiality with my duty to society.

Once, while I was in the process of recording details and assessing a client, he indicated, without remorse or empathy, that a few days before he had held a foreign student at knife point and taken her money and possessions. I was shocked. My empathy for the student and professional responsibility outweighed any confidentiality agreement. I informed him that I was terminating the interview in order to seek advice from my manager on the information he had just shared. The assessment was resumed a week later after the police had been informed. Throughout the client was kept aware of my actions.

A similar case presented itself when it was arranged for a social work student to shadow me for a day. His wife's car had been broken into during the night and the stereo stolen. Later that morning when the student and I were assessing a client and inquiring into how he funded his addiction, he informed us that he broke into cars and stole the stereos and radios in order to sell them.

As the lone specialist worker, I benefited from the opportunity of attending numerous multi-agency training workshops, conferences and seminars on drugs and alcohol; I also worked closely with agencies with specialist drugs and alcohol workers. I embarked on a programme of visiting the various social work teams during their team meetings to describe my role and to raise awareness of substance misuse services and to dispel some of the institutional attitudes and prejudices against clients with drugs or alcohol dependencies. I also began to work with our training department to begin facilitating basic awareness training on drugs and alcohol, similar to what I had done for HIV/AIDS. Later, I began to collaborate with our training department in planning and facilitating awareness training similar to that which I had pioneered in HIV/AIDS. Through my contact at Sussex University, I extended this awareness training to facilitating workshops for social work students.

Working in this specialist field, I witnessed first-hand the destructive impact of substance misuse on families, particularly in cases where children were the victims of their parents' lifestyles. I also recognised the impact on the wider community in terms of criminality and the cost to health and social care. All these activities and happenings would not have come to fruition had it not been for the support and understanding my manager gave me. One of the difficulties of being a specialist social worker is the isolation and having to work alone. At times when I needed support, either face to face or by phone, he would always make himself available.

Because of the increasing amount of managerial responsi-bility, I was given in the team, I was unofficially regarded by my colleagues as the assistant service manager as well as being the senior practitioner. It did not come as a surprise when Mike, my line manager, was promoted to area manager. I was approached, in March 1999, by the head of mental health services, Phil Mason, and asked to serve as acting service manager until the job was advertised. My appointment, albeit a temporary one, made another significant crack in the glass ceiling hanging over my head and was a positive step forward in achieving racial equality in the workplace.

As acting service manager for substance misuse and HIV/ AIDS services, I was directly accountable to the group manager and for a team of specialist workers across the county. My remit included budgetary responsibilities which made me aware of the high cost to the local authority of funding clients in residential rehabilitation centres and our financial position and statutory obligations in meeting demand. It became my responsibility to deal with this matter. This coincided with the debate being held at the time about cost and efficiency and whether community rehabilitation was more successful in the longer term than residential rehabilitation. To add to this, a best value review of the commissioning of residential rehab services had looked at the effectiveness, efficiency and quality of the service.

With my experience and qualifications, I decided to extend the best value review by carrying out a research analysis of the outcome for service users that we, the local authority, had funded in residential rehabilitation over a 12-month period. Funding for residential rehabilitation was for 13 weeks and was linked to the 12-step recovery programme. Each step was meant to last a week and the focus during the final week was preparing the client for reintegration into the community. Unfortunately, in reality, less than half of our clients completed the full 13 weeks.

My analysis was retrospective with data from a cross sample of 48 service users placed in residential establishments across Sussex in a particular calendar year; something that had never been done before. While the sample was predominantly white, male, single and aged 26 to 39, I was pleased that it also revealed an increase in the female ratio, one of my objectives when I was appointed senior practitioner. In my qualitative analysis, I looked at the duration of stay in residential rehabilitation against the following factors: gender, age, religion and marital status, clients with children, time of placement and the substance involved (alcohol or drugs). My analysis revealed some useful data, including that less than half of the clients (38%) completed the 13 weeks, with more than a quarter (27%) completing less than two weeks. More clients had been admitted for drugs than alcohol. There was also a correlation between the duration of stay and whether children were involved – and the former and the choice of rehabilitation accommodation.

Although my research analysis was qualitative and limited in making firm conclusions, it revealed a pattern and raised issues about residential rehabilitation. My findings were used by other statutory agencies involved in the funding of substance misuse clients in this area. Prior to my analysis, residential rehabilitation was viewed by the local authority as the solution. It was costly and less than half of the clients we funded completed the 13 weeks, as my data showed. Although community rehabilitation had a longer duration, it was less costly and had a higher success rate. As a matter of fact, most of the clients who had failed to complete the 13 weeks residential programme ended up being supported in the community. My research analysis resulted in additional resources being invested in community services and programmes to find alternatives to residential services. This benefitted those people who found it difficult to commit or adhere to a 13-week residential programme.

What I was advocating from my analysis was the need for community services. I was proud that my research had been acknowledged and that it had a practical application which was used and referred to in multi-agency meetings. It was a personal achievement for me to have provided concrete evidence that my team, in collaboration with other agencies, were achieving our objectives in funding and extending substance misuse services to women.

I was appointed to the position of acting service manager in 1999, with the assurance that the post would be advertised within a few months, which is normal procedure. However, in reality, I experienced an unusually long period in this position'. There were four extensions, each of a month, which came in the form of a memo from the personnel department stating that senior management had agreed to extend my position. The first memo came just a month after the initial appointment and was followed by a similar memo every other month. After more than six months, my frustration was beginning to show, not with the work, which I was still enjoying, but rather because the job had still not been advertised. This was rather unusual and led me to wonder whether institutional racism was preventing me from being appointed permanently to the position. It was embarrassing to me as my family, friends and colleagues were all asking me why the job had yet to be advertised. I finally requested a meeting with my line manager, Phil, and reminded him of the unusually long period of my secondment and that I was also carrying senior practitioner responsibilities. This seemed to work. Within a few weeks the job was advertised both internally and externally.

CHAPTER 13

A dream come true

AS PART OF THE INTERVIEW PROCESS for the service manager's post, applicants were required to prepare and deliver a presentation on an issue or topic related to substance misuse. During the period I spent in mental health services I encountered many service users who had alcohol-related problems. Similarly, while working in substance misuse services, I was also encountering service users with mental health problems. This was a difficult dilemma for professionals in isolating or identifying the service user's primary problem. There was also a multi-agency issue with funding: if the primary problem is mental health then the health authority would be responsible for funding care services and if the primary problem is substance misuse it would be the responsibility of adult social care to fund care services.

The phrase 'dual diagnosis' refers to service users with both mental health and substance misuse problems. Because of my interest and research on dual diagnosis I decided to do a Powerpoint presentation on the subject and to highlight the need for a coordinated multi-agency response in tackling what was a growing cause for concern. I also planned to make reference to the lack of appropriate treatment options and facilities for women.

The senior management team of social services was based at County Hall, Lewes, which we regarded as the seat of power; it was where the interview was being held. I had made the journey to Lewes numerous times for meetings with Phil, my line manager, and was aware of the fact that by car, the journey could be unpredictable in the morning due to traffic congestion and roadworks. Added to this, it was very difficult to park. To avoid the stress of this, I left Hastings an hour earlier than usual. The weather that morning was sunny but, unlike on previous journeys when I would enjoy listening to jazz, on this occasion I kept revising my presentation in my head and trying to anticipate the questions I would be asked.

In the end, I felt confident about my interview; the presentation generated a lot of discussions, too. Attitudes and policies had changed since my first interview, in 1981, and it pleased me to see that the issue of race or ethnicity was no longer raised or discussed in interviews, although I am positive it was on the minds of some of the panel members. Yet it seemed the interview was about competence and qualification, as it should have been.

Later that afternoon, I received the much-anticipated phone call from the chair of the interview panel offering me the job of Countywide Service Manager for HIV/AIDS and substance misuse services. It was to be effective from September 1999. It was a professional and a personal achievement and a career milestone. I had not just shattered but broken through the organisational glass ceiling to become the first Black service manager for a countywide resource in East Sussex. I was particularly proud of the fact that I would be regarded as a role model for the other, albeit few, aspiring Black professionals who had joined the organisation after me.

Realistically, I knew that this might be the highest position I would be able climb to despite my qualifications, as a Black person within the organisation. However, I was determined that this would not be the case. I was also aware of two things: that the higher up the organisation I went, the more I would be distancing myself from the very purpose for which I came into the profession – to make a difference through my direct work and intervention with clients; and also, that as a Black person, the higher up I went, the more I would be placed under an organisational microscope.

My appointment came at a time when changes were occurring in the way organisations and agencies worked together. Multi-agency partnership had become the buzz phrase, particularly in the establishment of community mental health teams (CMHT). The rationale and philosophy underpinning partnership working and inter-professional development centred round the belief that some services worked best when they were integrated and coordinated. A significant legal milestone was the 1999 Health Act, which came into force the following year. Section 31 of the Act encouraged the sort of partnership arrangement and working that I was leading in HIV/AIDS and substance misuse.

The Health Act gave NHS bodies and local authorities the flexibility to respond more effectively to clients' needs by joining up existing services or jointly developing new and coordinated ones with other organisations. This was seen as cost effective, and the legal framework became a significant milestone in the commissioning and delivery of services. Previously it had been acknowledged that the distinction and interface between health and social services was ill-defined and at times unclear to clients in terms of accountability and responsibility for service provision and delivery.

At the time of my secondment, I was aware that discussions were being held between health and social services in relation to the future management and coordination of countywide HIV and substance misuse services. Now, as the newly appointed service manager, it became my responsibility to take this dialogue further regarding partnership working and the pooling of budgets. I was under no illusion that in the discussions that were to follow the health authority would be the major stakeholder, simply because they held a significantly larger budget.

Having spent years developing my skills and knowledge

in both specialities, I was passionate about continuing in that professional arena. However, I realised during the subsequent negotiations and discussions that this was not going to happen and that potentially I could be left in the wilderness as far as my career went. As a social worker, my greatest personal satisfaction and successes had been in specialist social work, but my position as service manager for those services, HIV/ AIDS and substance misuse, would be defunct and at the time, in 2000, I had no immediate career plan.

After months of 'best value' negotiations, both authorities, health and social services, arrived at an agreement and a new arrangement was drawn up. Under the newly proposed arrangement, both authorities would pool their HIV budgets and commission the Terrence Higgins Trust to develop and deliver HIV/AIDS services. Similar arrangements would see substance misuse services transferred to the health authority. The implementation of this partnership relationship and transition was scheduled to be completed over a six-month period.

Having to relinquish my role was a sad phase in my career. Reflecting on the positives though, one of my proudest contributions was being able to make a difference in changing the attitudes of the people within my organisation through information sharing and working with our training department with basic awareness training and workshops. I was also proud to have been on the working group in writing the organisational policies and guidelines for HIV/AIDS in East Sussex.

The transition period for the handing over of HIV/ AIDS services coincided with another reorganisation and restructuring in social services. Within adult services, this involved the phasing out of all service managers' posts and the introduction of new practice managers across the county. Practice managers would be accountable to newly created operations managers. As expected, all service managers were required to apply for new posts.

When the various posts were advertised, I spent some time contemplating what I wanted to do. Other than my family, I did not feel there was anyone I trusted enough to seek advice and guidance from, given that most of my colleague managers in similar positions to me and were thinking about their careers. At the time, I was also planning to enrol part-time at the University of Sussex to do a doctorate in social work. My dilemma was how to choose between my studies and my desire and ambition to shatter another glass ceiling and become the first Black operations manager in East Sussex. My line manager at the time was the head of the health services. In recognising the work I had done during the meetings and negotiations with the health authority, he encouraged me to apply for the operation managers' posts.

Since several managerial posts were simultaneously adver-tised, service managers were requested to identify or specify the options or alternatives we would consider if unsuccessful in our first choice. The option which I identified was practice manager for the countywide asylum team. This was also a specialist team and, having previously had responsibilities for two countywide services, I wanted my career path to remain in specialised service management. I also planned to negotiate about pursuing my doctorate.

The interview for Operations Manager was straight forward and I felt that I had given a confident performance. Although I was disappointed to hear I had not been appointed to that role, I was pleased with the news that I would manage the local authority's new asylum team. And so began a new chapter in my career.

CHAPTER 14

'Your kind of people': asylum and the new racism

THE RECEPTIONIST INDICATED THAT THE WOMAN CALLING WAS IRATE and was demanding to speak directly to the manager of the asylum team. I accepted the call and began with the usual pleasantries before asking how I could help. There was a few seconds' pause and, without reciprocating my greeting, she proceeded to ask if we kept fingerprints of all the asylum seekers the local authority was supporting. When I politely inquired why she felt we needed to do this, she paused again before informing me that her home had been burgled over the weekend and that the burglar could only be an asylum seeker. She continued by saying that if we had fingerprints, she could pass them on to the police to identify the culprit. I suggested that if she had been burgled she should contact the police immediately.

Judging by the woman's attitude, I assumed that the few seconds' pause at the start of our conversation was probably due to my African accent. The animosity and venom with which she uttered her opinions about asylum seekers was astonishing. There was no sympathy, remorse or understanding for what we, the asylum team, were doing with destitute asylum seekers or that people seeking asylum generally don't have a choice.

As a specialist worker in the HIV/AIDS and substance misuse team, I had dealt with numerous external and internal prejudices against clients; however, none were on the scale and magnitude of those I experienced while working with asylum seekers. My new role included defending their rights and challenging some very personal as well as institutional prejudices and stereotypes from professionals both within and outside of my organisation.

I recall a chat I once had at a management training workshop with my predecessor, who had been delegated the responsibility of setting up and recruiting staff to the new asylum team. I had known her for some years and was aware of her various responsibilities in social services over the years. At the tea break she approached me and said that she wanted to pick my brain for advice 'about your kind of people'. I initially assumed that she was referring to either

HIV/AIDS or substance misuse until, then the penny dropped and I realised what she was alluding to my 'background'.

I politely asked why she thought, or had assumed, that I was an asylum seeker. This may have seemed a light-hearted remark to her as she didn't take it seriously. We both smiled and continued mingling with the other managers there. However, she had not only made an assumption about my background but had also singled me out as the only Black manager on that training workshop: I was not 'one of them'.

I was motivated to accept the responsibilities of managing the asylum team for a number of reasons. It had a countywide brief and it kept me in the area of social work I had come to enjoy: specialism. Asylum issues presented local authorities with enormous challenges. At the heart of our profession are its core values and beliefs, which include equality, diversity, anti-oppressive practice, dignity, respect and social justice. However, the Immigration and Asylum Acts struck at the heart of these values and principles in terms of race and immigration.

On a personal level, I had also had some experience of the process first-hand, having been forced with my wife and young children to migrate to the UK from war-torn Liberia in the early 1980s. As Karen and the children were British citizens, I avoided being given the label 'asylum seeker'. However, the initial restrictions imposed on my entry and the process for acquiring permanent resident status and later citizenship were no different from those applying to anybody seeking asylum in the UK during the 1980s.

Local authorities had become involved in this area of specialist work and intervention following the Balkan wars of the 1990s, which resulted in an influx of migrants initially into neighbouring countries, and then beyond into Western Europe. In the UK, several attempts were made by the government to discourage asylum seekers from entering the country. These started with the introduction of a number of stringent legislative changes, in particular the Immigration and Asylum Act 1999, entitled 'Fairer, Faster and Firmer'. This act introduced a series of drastic measures such as the dispersal of asylum seekers across the country away from London, the voucher system to replace cash benefits, changes to support arrangements and the removal of eligibility for asylum seekers to work.

Prior to the new Act, destitute asylum seekers had been supported by local authorities under the 1948 National Assistance Act. The 1999 Asylum Act transferred responsibility to the newly formed National Asylum Support Service (NASS) within the Home Office. Part IV of the Immigration and Asylum Act created interim regulations for local authorities to offer support only to destitute asylum seekers, and their families already in the United Kingdom who had applied for refugee status prior to 2000. In other words, the team existed for the specific purpose of clearing the backlog of asylum applications. The only exception to this arrangement was that unaccompanied asylum-seeking children remained the responsibility of social services departments.

Because generic social services teams did not have the

infrastructure and specialist knowledge for dealing with the large number of asylum seekers and their families, approval was granted to set up a specialist asylum team. The unit was inaugurated in June 2000 and I was its second practice manager. The financial cost of setting up and running the team, including my salary and the salaries of the staff, were funded by the Home Office which, for me, raised the issue of my social work duties and own accountability to the Home office. This arrangement also raised personal as well as professional conflicts for me in terms of the Home Office's expectations; it was technically my employer and its motivation and mandate was one of immigration control and the removal of failed asylum seekers from the UK – against my professional ethics and the core values of social services which I remained determined to uphold.

There were three phases to our work. The first involved the setting up of the necessary infrastructure and services to meet the diverse cultural, medical, accommodation and legal needs of asylum seekers who had arrived in the UK and applied for refugee status prior to 2000 and for whom the local authority were responsible. This phase had been successfully accomplished by my predecessor prior to my appointment.

My responsibility began with the implementation of the second phase, which included working directly with the Home Office and solicitors on asylum seekers' applications for refugee status. It was anticipated that this phase would take four years to complete. The Home Office hoped that within that timeframe they would have interviewed and arrived at a decision in respect of all our supported asylum seekers. The decision would be one of the following: indefinite leave to remain in the UK; exceptional (humanitarian) leave to remain for a specified period or a refusal of leave to remain in the UK. As a team, we were instructed to terminate all support within a month to asylum seekers who had received refusal letters and were unable to appeal against their decisions.

At the time of my appointment as practice manager, the local authority had responsibility for the welfare and support of approximately 150 destitute asylum seekers who were accommodated in public and privately owned premises across the county. Our primary obligations, as dictated by the Home Office, were to provide the families with services that met their basic needs, including financial support, access to immigration solicitors, advocacy, advice and liaison with other statutory and voluntary agencies. In terms of their demographic profile, they were predominantly male, single and mostly between the ages of 18 to 35. The majority were Kosovans, followed by Albanians, Turks, people from former Yugoslavia and Russians. A smaller number had come from countries in Africa.

Asylum seekers were required to report to the team weekly in order to receive their benefits and to update us with any developments from their solicitors regarding their asylum claims. During these weekly visits, I made it my duty to meet with as many of them as possible. I was keen to hear about their experiences and their story told by themselves and not the media. As they got to know me and my African roots from these informal chats, they were initially shocked, then proud to see a Black manager dealing with and responsible for their welfare. I think some of them, particularly the young men from Africa, began to see me as a kind of role model and a symbol of what they might achieve in England.

One of the cultural issues and difficulties we encountered were from some Muslim families regarding their attitude towards women: some wore the burka and were not allowed by their husbands to come to the office. We overcame this issue by allowing our female staff to visit them with their benefits and to confirm their identities at home.

Perhaps one of the greatest challenges I faced during that time was having to terminate support to asylum seekers who had received a final negative decision and a failed appeal from the Home Office on their asylum application. I remember an asylum seeker whose support services, including his accommodation, were being terminated by the local authority, asking me how I expected him to survive with neither money nor accommodation. It was an impossible question to answer from a social worker's perspective, but obviously not from that of the Home Office.

I had a lot of empathy for the asylum seekers and their experiences and my position in the team enabled me to get to know most of them. We found that most were cognisant of the public attitude towards them and how negatively the media was portraying them, as drains on the welfare system. Paradoxically, their immigration status prevented them from employment, which they wanted in order to be independent of public assistance while awaiting their Home Office decisions.

On a personal level, although my journey to the UK and circumstances were somewhat different from the asylum seekers we supported, we shared the common experience of having to leave our birth countries for political or military reasons. In my case, the military coup in Liberia and subsequent events precipitated my having to leave my home country with my family and start over. As a result of this commonality, I believe I was in an advantaged position as the team's manager to understand some of the verbal and non-verbal messages our clients frequently expressed, particularly in relation to separation and loss. That enabled me to talk to some of the asylum seekers about their personal safety, particularly the younger ones, and to advise them because of negative public attitudes to be careful where they visited or socialised in town. From my unique position, I could also challenge some asylum seekers on some of their cultural views, such as attitudes to women and what was acceptable and unacceptable in the UK.

At the beginning of the Balkan wars, public attitude towards asylum seekers was sympathetic and fairly accepting, but as increased numbers came to the UK, that perspective began to change. Asylum seekers were seen by some as having greater access to public and welfare services over the local population, fuelling racism and antagonism towards them generally.

Other immigrant groups had gone through similar experiences before. The way the Windrush generation and immigrants from Africa were treated led to an acknowledgement from the UK government that racial discrimination existed and that legal provisions were needed not only to remedy the situation, but to help achieve racial equality. One key piece of legislation was the Race Relations Act of 1976. This act was the first major acknowledgement by the government that personal and institutional racism existed which made it illegal and unacceptable to discriminate against ethnic minorities in a number of areas. The act outlawed discrimination in several areas including employment, provision of goods and services and housing. The Race Relations amendment act 2000, following the Macpherson inquiry and report into the murder of Steven Lawrence extended the coverage of the 1976 Act and placed a duty on all public authorities to promote equality of opportunities and good relations between people from different racial groups.

However, knowing that it was against the law to discriminate against a person based on their race, some people sought to exclude asylum seekers from these legislations, arguing that they were not yet British citizens and so not protected. Discrimination against asylum seekers in the UK became the new racism, played out on both institutional and personal levels. Discrimination against asylum seekers, including unaccompanied minors, was often played out in the language used against them in the media – why should the British public support them? Why didn't they just go back to their own countries?

Professor Arun Kundnani talks about the image of asylum

seekers being defined not by what they are, but more simply by the fact that they are, i.e. 'not one of us' and therefore a threat to 'our way of life'. He identifies two principal ways in which the state generated popular racism through the asylum system. The first principal he refers to as the 'logic of suspicion', whereby the Home Office, under pressure to reduce the burden of asylum claims, put obstacles in the way of members of this group, making it harder to obtain successful claims. I can personally identify with this in my own efforts and struggles to obtain British nationality in 1980, after I had to leave Liberia following the coup. The second principal is what he calls the 'logic of deterrence', where cruelty to asylum seekers seems permissible as a deterrent to stop others exploiting the asylum system. The Home Office thus created a hostile environment to prevent such 'exploitation'.

In the beginning, the team presented me with some unique challenges which I classified as 'internal' within the team and 'external' outside the organisation. These challenges manifested themselves in different ways at different times. The internal issues related to the departure of my predecessor and my arrival as her replacement when certain individuals in the team felt that they should have been appointed to the position. My new line manager was aware of the difficulties I was experiencing and was very supportive of me in dealing with the issue which was noticeably affecting the morale of the team.

Although comparatively smaller than other teams in social services, it was also atypical in that most of the staff were either from minority ethnic groups or had connections to them through marriage or other relationships. From my observations at conferences and external meetings, there was generally an overwhelming number of ethnic minority staff working with asylum seekers. I began to wonder if this area genuinely appealed to minority ethnic professionals or whether we were being driven into it by our organisations and agencies. In my case, for example, it had not been my first choice to manage the asylum team. It seemed somewhat strange that minority groups, which historically and traditionally had lacked power and organisational influence, were now effectively empowering and advocating on behalf of another powerless group of people, asylum seekers, who were also facing similar discrimination.

I was surprised by my initial experiences with my team, although they were similar to the experiences expressed by other Black managers at an asylum conference I had attended in London. In the course of our discussions, a number of them indicated that they were being undermined by other Black professionals in their teams, who were competing for the same recognition or opportunity to crack the glass ceiling.

Another issue was to do with lack of training and knowledge. The asylum team was located on the ground floor of a multi-storey building shared by other services, including adult social care, professionals and a pool of administrative workers. I shared an office on the tenth floor with another manager. One day, one of the receptionists came to my office to tell me that 'a foreign looking gentleman' was in reception and wondered whether she should refer him to the asylum team. When I asked her if the gentleman was an asylum seeker, she said she didn't know. It transpired that she had not even spoken to the gentleman but had simply concluded that he was non-white and looked foreign and therefore must have been an asylum seeker. Later that day, I met with the receptionist to revisit the issue and the assumptions she had made about a client. Our meeting was fruitful and she agreed that it was an issue for awareness training which she felt was lacking in the department and would be useful for frontline staff.

Challenging attitudes through training was the answer to overcoming the prejudices and commonly held stereotypes about asylum seekers. I had succeeded with introducing awareness training on HIV/AIDS and substance misuse and therefore my next objective and focus became awareness training on asylum and our legal duties and responsibilities. I opened a dialogue with our training department. Given that this is a specialist area of asylum work, I gained the interest and participation of our legal department, as well as from solicitors and other agencies who were working with asylum seekers. I extended this training to Sussex Police. Between April and August 2001, I was asked by Sussex Police to assist in their training of officers on the subjects of race and asylum, and for this I was awarded a certificate by the police in recognition of my assistance to them.

In planning to facilitate workshops with social services staff, I started recording some of the negative comments and statements about asylum seekers made in my presence by social work colleagues. These included:

'Why should we, the British taxpayer, have to support them?'

'They are all cheats, trying to fiddle the system.'

'They can't be that destitute, walking around with mobile phones.'

What I did at the start of each workshop was to display the statements on PowerPoint and then ask participants to discuss in small groups the person or persons to whom they would have attributed the statements. As I moved around the groups, listening to their discussions, the answers I heard were from anything from the media to racist groups or organisations. There was total disbelief and denial when I informed them that the statements had been made by colleagues and professionals within our organisation. Their attitudes and prejudices reflected those of the general public, and I was pleased that the training workshops created a positive shift in beliefs and attitudes among staff.

I became involved in many multi-agency and regional groups to focus on the welfare and education of asylum seekers. This was an area of work in which I felt comfortable and knowledgeable. Some of the multi-agencies had the monitoring remit of the immigration status of asylum seekers in their regions. In most of these meetings, I seemed to have the dual task of defending the rights of asylum seekers as well as dealing with the prejudices directed towards them from the public and some professionals, including professionals in the asylum team. I recall having to have strong words with a team member during a meeting in which she stated that she could always tell when asylum seekers were lying because their lips did not move.

Because not everyone on the team was a qualified social worker, it was my practice to give them some experience by taking them to multi-agency meetings. One particular such meeting was held in Dover, its aim to discuss ways of pooling our collective resources and creating a database of information. Dover was a significant venue given that the port was one of the gateways into the UK for asylum seekers. The meeting was being hosted by the local authority asylum team there.

When we arrived at the office, I introduced myself and my male resource officer to the receptionist who indicated that her manager was expecting me. She rang the manager to inform him of our arrival. After a few minutes, a white man came through a door into the reception area where my colleague and I were standing. He went straight to my colleague, who was white, and greeted him as 'Mr Johnson'. When I indicated that I was Mr Johnson, he was unable to contain his embarrassment at his error. Looking back, what surprised me more was that during our journey back to Hastings, when I mentioned the manager's assumption, his action had not even registered with my colleague. This experience was one that was repeated many times during my social work career.

Of the various agencies set up by the Home Office to deal with asylum issues on its behalf, I felt that the local authority was ideal for that task. Social work is perhaps one of the few caring professions that place equality, social justice and anti-oppressive practice at the core of its principles and values. Working with asylum seekers put those principles and our commitment to them to the test. People who harbour negative attitudes and prejudices towards asylum seekers may never have taken the time to look beyond the media portrayal of this group in order to fully understand their situation and why people would put their lives at risk trying to reach the safety offered by another country.

Two years into my post with the asylum team, an opportunity of a different nature arose, one which I found irresistible. The Social Work Department at the University of Sussex was advertising for a part-time social work tutor on their masters' social work programme. The advert indicated that two social workers could share the part-time post for two years.

After consultation with my manager, I forwarded my application to the university and was offered the secondment in a job-share with another practitioner who, at the time, was studying for his doctorate. I believe that what impressed the university was my general social work experience. I was already known at the university as a consultant and advisor to Black social work students, as well as a visiting lecturer on race matters. I felt that my experiences were also important considerations for the university.

The secondment was without a doubt an exciting and memorable phase in my career. I had satisfied a goal to go into social work education and training, as well as having cracked another glass ceiling. There were no other Black lecturers on the faculty who could act as role models or mentors. I was happy and proud as a Black tutor to fulfil those roles for the few Black and minority ethnic social work students on the programme and also to have been partly instrumental in having race and diversity issues reflected in the academic programme.

My job-share colleague and I had an office at the university; it meant that I usually had it to myself two days a week. Observing the names and titles on office doors, I could not avoid noticing that most of the lecturers were 'doctors' – my job-share colleague was studying for his doctorate and would soon also have that title on the door to our office. It seemed that having a doctorate degree not only represented academic authority, it also bestowed on the holder feelings of membership of an elitist group. I was determined to join that club.

At the end of my first year there, I enrolled on the part-time doctorate programme in social work at the university. It was a heavy commitment in addition to work, not to mention the disruption to my family life. As a doctorate student, my Friday evenings and Saturday mornings were spent in lectures. I also had a full-time job commitment to the asylum team.

Towards the end of 2004, the team had achieved the objectives set under the interim arrangements and the Home Office could not justify having a full asylum resource. The third and final stage of our operation involved the gradual transfer of our remaining cases back to the Home Office and facilitating the redeployment of my staff. It was sad knowing that as a team we were nearing the end of our existence. It was also distressing for the remaining asylum seekers, many of whom we had built trust and confidence with only to lose our support.

I have tried to understand what led me to the asylum team, especially when it appeared that other managers seemed uninterested in that area of social work. To a large extent, I think I was happy to have played a key role in the process of change and in steering the team through its objectives. Together, we managed to change some negative attitudes and stereotypes about asylum seekers and more importantly, we made a difference for many of those young people who were destitute, away from their countries and families and in need of our help and support.

A few months prior to the final phase, when staff redeployment was on the agenda, I received a telephone message from my senior manager. The practice manager for the sensory impairment team was retiring and I was encouraged to consider the post. Both personally and professionally, the thought of managing another specialist team was appealing. News of my interest spread, and I was approached by some of the social workers working there who stated how pleased they were to hear the news. I was also contacted by the departing practice manager of the sensory impairment team for an informal meeting. That meeting turned out to be most uncomfortable for both of us. It seemed she was being forced to take retirement and as a result she had decided to fight against the decision.

After several months of senior management procrastination, I was again contacted by my senior manager, who presented me with a short-term job option while awaiting the sensory impairment team job – to act as a practice manager in an 'advisory capacity' to the organisation on HIV/AIDS and asylum issues. This new advisory role was ill-defined and clearly had not been thought through and I was able to use that period of uncertainty to focus on my doctorate studies while things worked themselves out.

A few months into the advisory role, I was presented with another 'carrot' while still awaiting the move to the sensory impairment team. This time it was a temporary appointment as practice manager for the out-of-county placement team within the countywide learning disability team based in Eastbourne.

PART 5

MY WILDERNESS YEAR

CHAPTER 15

Learning disability services

*'I always believe that you can think positive
just as well as you can think negative.'*

James Baldwin

AFTER TWELVE MEMORABLE AND PRODUCTIVE
YEARS as a practitioner and manager for HIV/AIDS and
substance misuse services, plus a further four years with
the asylum team, I was enticed into leaving the comfort and
security of those services that I had developed, and with
which my name had become closely associated, to take up a
temporary post with the out-of-county placement team within
learning disability services in Eastbourne. By that stage in
my career with East Sussex Social Services, I had seen and
experienced many reorganisations and had an awareness of the
internal organisational politics in social services. Nevertheless
I accepted the move, albeit with a great deal of scepticism

and reluctance. Learning disability was perhaps the only area of social work I had not experienced. As a practice educator and mentor, I thought the new experience would enhance my profile.

The enticement used by senior management was that this would be a temporary move and that they wanted my skills and experience of working alongside another manager, who was also being transferred to learning disabilities to 'sort out the team'. I accepted the move in good faith, believing that my post with the sensory impairment team was still on the cards. The assurance I had was contained, not in the usual formal letter, but instead in an email between my line manager at the time and the Head of Disabilities Services, dated 27 May 2005, which had been copied to both me and to the assistant director of adult social care. It read:

> *I have had the opportunity of talking to James about the temporary management of the Residential Place-ment Team and he is keen to accept the challenge. I have explained that this would be expected to take a maximum of half his full-time post and that it would be temporary up to December 2005.*

What made this proposal more appealing was the indication that the job would take half my full-time post, and as the local authority no longer had an asylum team, despite the fact that both adult and children services were still dealing with asylum issues, I was asked to be a consultant and an adviser to the authority on asylum issues. This would account for the other half of my post.

In retrospect, I was rather naïve and had not yet learned lessons from the earlier experiences of institutional racism. My scepticism had to do with the fact that the practice manager whose post I would be taking, albeit temporarily, had suddenly been made redundant. My new team had not been given any information about her departure nor of my arrival. To add to this confusion, another senior team manager, Paula, had already been brought in as a temporary caretaker manager from her previous role as complaints manager, based at County Hall, Lewes.

The residential placement team, RPT, was one of several teams within learning disability services and its primary duties involved the monitoring and reviewing of high-cost placements across Sussex and beyond. Although the team was also charged with the responsibility of monitoring low-cost placements, the primary focus and target was on high cost ones. On reflection and against my better judgement, I jumped at the idea and the new challenge. Like the sensory impairment services, this presented a new area of specialism and I had limited knowledge of how social services responded to the needs of clients with severe learning disabilities and sensory impairment. A more important reason was that I thought the move and experience would be an added bonus and experience for managing the sensory impairment team. It would also boost my own confidence and profile as a specialist practitioner. Accepting this new and temporary challenge would entail relocating again from Hastings to Eastbourne and having to leave home earlier in the morning and return later in the evening.

The RPT consisted of a qualified social worker, two resource officers and an administrative assistant. Unfortunately for me, the team did not have a senior practitioner. Suffice it to say those involved did not welcome the arrival of two new managers. They harboured some anger and suspicion over the manner in which their previous manager, to whom they were very close, had been ousted, fuelling rumours about their own future and that of their team.

Initially Paula and I began to work well together and had a good understanding of our new remit while striving to make the best of a bad situation. We also succeeded in gaining the confidence of the staff through our honesty and regard for their welfare and security. We achieved this through our open communication.

Unlike Paula, one of the inconveniences I encountered as a manager involved having to work in an open-plan office with more than 50 professionals, including the RPT. I had no access to a direct telephone and no privacy for storing documents or information relating to the team. It felt humiliating, particularly as Paula enjoyed the luxury and privacy accorded to all the managers in the learning disability services. As the only Black manager and worker in that service I felt visible in a negative way. I accepted the working conditions because of the assurance I had been given that the move was temporary. Institutional racism had once again reared its ugly head and I was being marginalised.

I understood and it made sense that as an out-of-county team, my staff would be expected to spend considerable time away from the office, travelling and carrying out reviews and assessments, but I had not anticipated the degree and extent to which it happened. For the first two weeks the only people in the team I saw were Paula and our administrative assistant. I began to conclude that the workers were deliberately avoiding coming to the office by planning their daily journeys from home to their destination. I decided to exert my authority by inviting all the staff to attend a meeting at the office in order to arrange team meetings and supervision dates and times. Ironically, I was planning to book formal supervision sessions without an office where I could close the door.

The RPT was located on the fifth floor of a multi-storey building in Eastbourne. Also accommodated in the building were other teams, including mental health, adult social care and children services. An advantage for me of being seated in an open-plan office among a range of other professionals was the opportunity to overhear some of the negative comments made about my team in general and about some of the workers in particular. I was particularly disappointed to hear some comments which were unfair and unkind, and I challenged other managers about this, albeit with limited success as it seemed minds had already been made up about the team.

Establishing one-to-one supervision meetings with team members proved valuable in building relationships and acquiring a flavour of their individual activities. This paved the way for me to introduce some structure and planning to their work and the placement review process. My next step was to travel to some of the out-of-area residential establishments and to take the lead in chairing reviews.

I introduced a rota system which required at least one worker to remain in the office to deal with emergencies. These measures were welcomed by the team, who also engaged with monthly staff meetings at the office. It was challenging to introduce structure to a team which appeared to have been without it for a considerable time. Although I anticipated some initial resistance to the changes I was implementing, after a short period my relationship with the team began to improve and my staff understood that they could trust my honesty.

After visiting a number of our most expensive residential placements, I began to make my assessment and analysis of what these services provided vis-à-vis their high cost. In some of the placements, I had serious doubts about the quality of their services and whether they provided good value for money. It was frustrating, for now we had no alternative but to contract these resources out of area and regularly review their services. I shared my concerns and observations with Paula who was supportive and understanding of our task and the decisions we had to make. We had a good and positive working relationship. I kept her appraised of my progress and she understood the magnitude of what we had been tasked to achieve and the limited resources at our disposal. Working together we endeavoured to make the best with the limited resources available to us.

This working relationship and dynamics changed with the arrival of Sandra, another operations manager from County Hall to whom Paula and I would be accountable. Although Sandra's base was at County Hall, she began spending practically all of her working hours in Eastbourne. I had worked with Sandra in earlier years when she was a staff officer involved in training, including HIV/AIDS awareness training. Although I was never officially told, I discovered later that her brief included a value for money evaluation of the effectiveness of the out-of-county team, and that my brief was to work with her in achieving this objective. Rumours were circulating that the new team of managers had been sent in to close the RPT.

Sandra and I had worked together in a previous setting; however in this particular service there was a professional and personality clash between us to the extent that I felt she was often trying to undermine my authority within the team and also the decisions I made. One particular incident demonstrated this.

Prior to her arrival, I had received approval from personnel to fill a vacancy in the RPT and it had been further agreed with personnel that the process would begin internally through secondment to the team. I completed all the necessary groundwork for this recruitment and kept Paula informed, but from a number of conversations I had with Sandra, I sensed that while she wanted the vacancy to be filled, she wanted to take the credit for its outcome. She deliberately used her internal contacts and influences to delay the secondment in order to appear to have the final say. This led to a rather ugly and unpleasant argument between us in the presence of the team, which ended with her having to back down. Sadly for me, Paula, with whom I had worked well, took her side and began to distance and isolate herself from me.

As an established Black professional with years of credit for what I had achieved in my specialist field, I felt that this was an attempt by the organisation through these two managers to prevent my career moving any further and into the sensory impairment team. In addition to this I was now experiencing a gender problem: a female head of disability services, Debbie, plus Paula and Sandra, who were all close friends and had worked together in the past. I began to think of possible reasons why the previous female practice manager of the team had been made redundant and why I had been brought in.

The culture in the learning disability team had gradually become hierarchical and autocratic. This played out during our weekly funding panel meetings, which were attended by all managers who presented and supported applications on behalf of their team. These weekly funding panel meetings were chaired by Debbie, the head of services, and attended by all the practice managers, senior practitioners, and representatives from the finance section. The purpose of funding had to do with financial management in the allocation of resources and care packages to clients. Each manager had to present and justify their team applications for funding. I had encountered a similar funding panel as manager of HIV/AIDS and substance misuse services. What was also different was that at these weekly meetings, the residential placement team frequently became the butt of jokes and high-cost placements. I never got support from Paula or Sandra in responding to the wisecracks about my applications and the RPT.

In comparison to other teams, I felt that my funding applications were regularly subjected to greater scrutiny and more frequently postponed, ostensibly due to the lack of funding, until the following week or even later. I felt some of these were personal and at the end of each panel meeting I walked away feeling frustrated and unsupported and with empathy for the workers in the RPT who had put considerable time into their travels and assessments. I had been around long enough to recognise the organisational games that were being played and knew the length some colleagues would go to in order to further their careers and in setting others up to fail. Without having anyone to confide in, it was like being in the wilderness, professionally devalued and being let down by Paula who I had previously admired and trusted. The RPT had already sensed the atmosphere and division within the structure of the team.

My strategy for dealing with being marginalised and Isolated was to turn my focus away from the management to supporting the workers in the team. I began to accompany them more frequently on their visits out of Sussex. By engaging in this activity with my team I acquired valuable insight and understanding about clients with learning disabilities and the spectrum of their disabilities that necessitated the need for residential care. This knowledge enabled me to me more articulate during funding panel meetings.

Despite the positive thinking and optimism which I brought to the team, events had clouded that optimism and my thoughts were beginning to turn negative. Against my better judgement and in good faith, I had been persuaded to accept the transfer with the understanding that I would manage the sensory impairment team. Fifteen months later, nothing had changed and all communications with me regarding the sensory impairment team seemed to have ceased. My understanding was that the manager of the impairment team was involved in a dispute with the authority over her proposed redundancy.

The uncertainty of all this began to affect my health, in particular my blood pressure. At times, I regretted my decision to transfer to RPT and became angry with myself for being naïve. My motivation and enthusiasm began to wane and I began to despise the morning journeys to Eastbourne. The glass ceiling to me had become frosted. After twenty-five memorable years with East Sussex Social Services and having achieved most of what I wanted through my specialisms, I began to seriously explore my career options, even though at that stage in my career and in the current culture of the organisation, I knew the options were limited.

A number of senior managers had taken redundancies only to return six to eight weeks later as consultants in the same capacity, albeit with reduced hours. As my specialist posts, HIV/AIDS and asylum, no longer existed, I decided to have a formal meeting with the Assistant Director of Social Services about a similar redundancy package. I had come to know him well over the years and had worked with him on some projects relating to the substance misuse services. During our meeting, he indicated that I was 'too valuable' to the organisation to be made redundant. While this may have been intended by him as a compliment, I did not regard it as such, not least because I knew of the redundancy packages which had been awarded to managers much higher up the organisational tree.

Following the outcome and my disappointment over the meeting with the assistant director, I requested a formal meeting with my union representative for advice and guidance. Initially my union representative had led me to believe that I had a good chance of securing a redundancy package. However, during our second meeting, his position and advice to me seemed to have shifted. His language and advice were now similar if not identical to that of the assistant director, leaving me in no doubt that communication between the two had taken place. I was disappointed after paying my union subscription for so many years to find them unhelpful and impotent in dealing with senior management.

My final move involved a formal meeting with our personnel department. My specific agenda was the Local Government Pension Scheme, Rule 85. This rule was satisfied if an employee's age at the date they drew their benefit and the length of their scheme membership added up to 85 or more. This rule made it possible for employees to qualify for full benefits at a younger age. At the age of 60 and with over 25 membership years, I fully met the criteria. I was also aware that a number of employees had taken advantage of this rule.

My meeting with personnel was more productive than I had anticipated and I was provided with figures for my entitlement if I decided to pursue retirement through the 85-year rule. I was rather disappointed to discover that what was meant to have been a private and confidential meeting between personnel and myself soon became public knowledge, although none of my colleagues directly raised the issue with me to explore my feelings. The process could be described as an obstacle course in which my efforts were being hindered and my health was further affected.

Ultimately, I concluded that I had assembled enough information to inform my decision. Several months earlier, I had taken a break from my doctorate studies due to the pressures and stresses directly attributed to stress and isolation at work. Returning to complete my doctorate was one of my future options for life after social work.

In the final analysis and, after a lot of soul-searching and deliberation, I met again with the assistant director; this time I informed him of my desire to retire from the local authority under Rule 85. I formalised my letter of resignation immediately after our meeting and was flattered by his response that because of my contributions over the years, social services would make all efforts to have me back as a consultant.

Notifying the local authority on 2 March 2007 of my wishes to seek early retirement was liberating and I felt as though a heavy load had been lifted from my shoulders. My letter to the Assistant Director (Operations) read:

> 'As discussed at our recent meeting, I am now formally informing you of my wish to seek retirement at the end of June 2007'… 'I can reflect on my experience and the challenges of the past twenty-six years with fondness and gratitude to the many colleagues and service users who made that possible. I would like to thank you for your recent assistance and for the interest and support you have shown over the years in the specialist areas of work for which I had responsibility (e.g. asylum, HIV/AIDS).'

> His response read: '… I would like to take this opportunity to thank you for all your hard work over the past 26 years and your contribution to service improvement across a range of specialist areas.'

After a frustrating time, I now had a clear plan for my future. I had three months to serve out my notice and during that period I was flooded with good luck messages from friends and colleagues, many expressing hope for my return. Among the many messages were those from Black colleagues and workers expressing support and thanks for the work I had done and the support I had given them over the years. I had cracked the glass ceiling several times over. Now I was ready to move on and face new opportunities.

CHAPTER 16

A happy exit

"We mean to do right by you, but you've got to know your place at all times"

RALPH ELLISON

THE BIG QUESTION FOR ME FOLLOWING MY RESIGNATION was how I would spend my final three months with social services. It felt like another new experience. Clearly, I still had a job commitment as a practice manager in learning disability and consultant on asylum. At least now I felt I was able to carry out these challenging commitments with less stress and frustration simply because I could see light at the end of the tunnel. There was also a pervading feeling of sadness in leaving a struggling team, facing its own uncertainties, which had come to value my support and empathy.

When the news of my retirement was made public, I found time to reflect on the past twenty-five years. I wondered if without the glass ceiling I might have progressed higher up the organisational ladder. Some of my closest colleagues and friends opined that this was a certainty. As a Black social worker from the 1980s to early 2000s in a predominantly white organisation, I shared that view and perhaps should not have been frustrated by invisible barriers. I had had a memorable career.

Friday 29 June 2007 was a day I shall never forget, and perhaps one I will always cherish. It began with a drive to the county transport depot, some 30 miles from Hastings, to Ringmer, a town near Lewes in East Sussex. There were only two reasons to go there: either to sign an agreement for a leased car or to terminate an agreement and return the car. The purpose of my journey fell into the latter category. For the first time in more than fifteen years I would suddenly be carless. One of the workers in the residential placement team had kindly agreed to meet me at the depot for the journey back to the office in Eastbourne.

Returning to the office, I was greeted with a surprise. Paula had organised a farewell party for me at midday and had invited other social work teams. Given my experiences with the management team over the months, it was a surprise to me. They obviously seemed to have put the past behind them, and so had I. Following the customary speeches, gifts and cards, I became a little emotional in my thank you and farewell message to the team.

Just prior to the party, I was aware that my name and details had already been deleted from the computer system. I handed in my identification badge and my swipe card. Still slightly choked and overcome with emotion, I said my final goodbyes, bringing a career spanning a quarter of a century to a close.

Karen had travelled to Eastbourne to give me a ride back home to Hastings. Although the journey back felt liberating, I could not help reflecting on that summer's day in 1981 when, not having a car, I had found myself having to walk almost three miles from my home to Old Roar House for an informal interview to be a social care worker.

Over my career, I made many genuine friends and had the privilege of managing several superb specialist teams. I also felt fortunate to have been supervised by some very good managers. It felt appropriate to honour and say thanks to them in my own way, by hosting a leaving buffet party that evening at a public venue in Hastings. I was accompanied by Karen and our children, Michael and Michelle. It was an honour for me to see such a large turnout of former colleagues.

What impressed me the most was that among my guests were a number of Black social workers and practice managers who had joined the local authority after me. In his farewell speech, one of my Black colleagues referred to me as their 'trailblazer' and 'mentor'. I had cracked the glass ceiling, thereby giving them hope in their own careers.

In my remarks, I made reference to one of my favourite books, *Invisible Man* by the Black American author Ralph

Ellison, published in the early 1950s. Ellison writes about the intellectual issues facing Black Americans in the early twentieth century. Despite their achievements, Ellison stated that Black people lived in a society and culture in which they were socially invisible. In the course of my career I did at times experience this invisibility and was made to have an awareness of my place at time. Overall, there had been some positive progress, which I gradually experienced over the years and for which I fought to achieve to pave the way for Blacks and other minority groups entering the profession. I was proud to have made a difference and to have facilitated bringing about the change.

Four months after my departure I, together with many other newly retired county council employees, was invited to County Hall in Lewes and honoured at a reward ceremony. We were thanked for our service. It was another high point, marked with a group photo, and, just like that, the curtain came down on my career in East Sussex social services. It was a happy exit!

PART 6

EMBRACING THE NEW:
LIFE BEYOND SOCIAL SERVICES

CHAPTER 17

At the crossroads

A FEW YEARS PRIOR TO MY RETIREMENT, I had concluded that my attempts at cracking the glass ceiling in social services had hit a plateau. There were invisible barriers and I was not part of the established social group and network. Climbing the organisational ladder for me meant more than just doing a good job. My personal experience was that career progression for a Black social worker at the time was constrained by an invisible glass ceiling. I was established at the University of Brighton as a visiting lecturer, consultant and practice educator and had built-up a substantial professional network.

Throughout my career with the local authority I was actively involved in Black and ethnic minority issues, because I felt they needed to be kept on the local agenda. I served as chairman for Hastings and Rother Black and ethnic minority forum from 1994 to 1996 and in that role, in 1995, I also chaired a multi-agency research steering group looking at the needs of these communities. An external researcher was commissioned and the outcome and conclusions, entitled 'Listen in Silence', was published in 1996. It provided valuable local and regional information. I was proud to have chaired the group and to have my name and role in the report.

However, my immediate plan was to take a short break to re-energise myself. I had a number of options after retiring from social services at the age of 60 and now I was contemplating what I might do next – become a freelance lecturer, practice educator, independent advisor to Sussex Police, complete my PhD or pursue something new and challenging in social work. High on my priority options and plan was the completion of the final phase of the doctorate from which I taken a break because of the combined pressure of juggling work with studies.

One of the areas that interested me was that of asylum seekers with special needs, an umbrella phrase which referred to those individuals with mental health problems, physical disabilities or some other health related problems such as HIV/AIDS. Through my studies, I discovered that existing research literature on this group had mainly been concerned with mental health or issues associated with migration. HIV/AIDS had been comparatively overlooked. I wanted my thesis to enlighten professional understanding of asylum seekers with HIV.

The working title of my thesis was 'Living with uncertainties'. Although asylum seekers generally felt unsafe because of the events in the countries that led them to seek refuge in the UK, many with HIV/AIDS faced discrimination and uncertainties in gaining access to vital services including healthcare. It was the nature of their experiences and the professional responses to them that I had proposed to make the subject of my research. I wanted to explore the experiences directly from the asylum seekers' point of view rather than from the perspective of the concerns and difficulties experienced by the statutory and voluntary agencies dealing with them. I had spent several months interviewing and gathering information from asylum seekers with HIV/AIDS, professionals working in the HIV/AIDS field and the organisations which supported destitute asylum seekers.

My involvement with Sussex Police in training and consultancy had begun two years earlier in early 2001 when, as practice manager for the local authority asylum team, I was asked to facilitate the training of its officers, raising awareness of race issues and examining negative attitudes, stereotypes and assumptions about Black people. I had always understood that the request for me to be part of this training was based first and foremost on my position as a Black man and not on my profession or experience.

The focus of the training was on street intervention and the implementation of 'stop and search'. The 1984 Police and Criminal Evidence Act gave police officers the power to stop an individual and carry out a search if there were reasonable grounds for suspicion that articles unlawfully obtained or possessed were being carried and that the articles were likely to be found during the search. 'Reasonable grounds for suspicion' are based on the experience and judgement of the officer and the circumstances of each case. However, reasonable grounds can be subjective and, in some cases, supported by personal factors like race and gender. I have always been a believer and advocate for 'stop and search' as an effective police tool for dealing with crime; however, that police power was frequently criticised for the disproportionality of its use in Black and minority ethnic communities. This was what concerned me and my local police force were keen to learn how they could begin to engage meaningfully with the different ethnic minorities groups in the community. With the consent of East Sussex social services, I delivered the training and consultancy over a six-month period. Witnessing their participation and involvement in the training, I felt that there was a genuine desire among police officers to manage race matters more appropriately. The sessions were well evaluated by the participants.

The training and awareness sessions were happening as a consequence of the 1999 MacPherson Report into the Stephen Lawrence murder inquiry. Lawrence was a Black teenager murdered by a group of young white men in south London six years earlier. The report concluded that the investigation into his murder had been 'marred by a combination of professional incompetence, institutional racism and a failure of leadership'. It criticised the Metropolitan Police Service for its loss of contact with local communities, particularly Black communities, and challenged the police service to start a process of genuine partnership with them. Independent Advisory Groups, known as IAGs, evolved to facilitate that partnership and engagement, and to act as 'critical friends', offering independent advice and feedback in relation to police service delivery. In response, Sussex police developed a network of IAGs operating at the strategic and divisional levels.

The Macpherson Report also examined police powers and their use of 'stop and search'; it asserted that Black people were several times more likely to be stopped and searched by the police than those who were white. According to police statistics nationally, a Black man was 26 per cent more likely to be stopped and searched by the police. This figure was not a surprise to me: it existed in other authorities and disciplines. During my mental health training, I became aware that Afro-Caribbeans were three times more likely to be admitted or detained compulsorily under the Mental Health Act and were prescribed higher doses of medication to control their behaviour. Similar evidence from the criminal justice system revealed that Blacks and Asians were more likely to receive a prison sentence than a white counterpart convicted of the same offense.

Not long after the training sessions, I was awarded a certificate at a special police ceremony and later was asked to consider becoming a strategic independent advisor. Given the Black community's lack of trust and confidence in the police, particularly at the time of Macpherson and its subsequent recommendations, I felt that I needed to consider the added value my ethnicity could bring to the role – and also how that position and my professional relationship with the police might be perceived and interpreted by the local Black community. I was particularly mindful that I would not accept being used by the police force as a 'tick box' for consultation with the Black community.

After careful consideration and consultation with close friends and Black colleagues, I concluded that the only way to effect change and make a true difference was from the inside and so I accepted the role of 'critical friend' to the force. I helped it to build insight into the needs, wants and voice of Black and minority ethnic groups who were under-represented in their existing decision-making process. At times my role necessitated having to challenge some of the traditional policies and ways the force operated.

As a strategic independent advisor, I became a member of a subgroup, the street intervention accountability group, which met monthly to scrutinise stop and search figures and to scrutinise its application.

In addition to this, during the second week of my break, I came across an advert in the local paper for a palliative care social worker job at the local hospice. After spending the past eight years in management, there was a part of me that was keen to return to complete my career, just as it had begun: delivering hands-on social work to clients and service users. I had considered working in a different, challenging area of social work, and now it seemed the opportunity had arisen.

I forwarded my application and was invited to attend an interview. To help prepare for it, I had an informal conversation with a member of the hospice staff with whom I had previously worked. She gave me a balanced view of the hospice, stating that in terms of patient care, it was second to none.

The interview went well, even though the all-female inter-view panel, two managers and manager of human resources was my first cultural shock. This would never have occurred in social services, where a token male at least would have been included in the panel. Following the interview though, I was offered the job. It suited me that it was a part-time post and I could therefore continue my freelance training and consultancy work, including working as a practice educator to social work students. It was a win-win situation for me.

As a Liberian, the thought of being referred to as 'doctor' was attractive, the title carrying a lot of social and economic kudos. Sadly though, in the end it was not to be. I had chosen not to pursue medicine and at the time of writing this my PhD remains uncompleted. I had put my studies on the back burner for a year, and with the new career challenges ahead, I finally withdrew from my studies. It was not an easy decision, but I eventually rationalised it by convincing myself that being titled 'Dr' was not everything in life.

I also retired as a countywide strategic independent advisor and became an independent divisional advisor for Hastings instead, where the focus was on local operational matters rather than policies at the countywide level. Yet I felt I could do more.

CHAPTER 18

Journey into palliative care

*'How people die remains in the memories of
those who live on.'*

DAME CICELY SAUNDERS

DURING MY SOCIAL WORK TRAINING IN THE EARLY
1980s, palliative or end-of-life care was absent from the
curriculum because it was regarded a medical or nursing
issue. The training did include topics on separation and loss
and the effects on children who were away from their birth
parents for a variety of reasons. Death was a taboo subject.

My introduction to end-of-life care was through the work
of Elisabeth Kübler-Ross, the American psychiatrist who,
in 1969, published her seminal book *On Death and Dying*,
identifying five stages of coping with terminal illness. The

objective of the 2010 National Framework 'Supporting people to live and die well: a framework for social care at the end of life' was to identify and raise awareness of the role of social care in supporting people at their end of life. The framework revealed that social care staff lacked confidence in this area of work and felt that end-of-life care was not an issue for them. Even with all the social work skills and experiences that we acquired in dealing with difficult issues and situations, when it came to handling any discussion about death or dying, we lacked confidence. Social workers are trained to work in many situations concerned with loss, so social work practice and skills had much to offer in end-of-life care.

The hospice movement, as we know it today, was established by Dame Cicely Saunders in 1967. Although Dame Cecily was a doctor, she was also trained in social work. My own contact with hospices began in the early 1990s when I was working as an HIV/AIDS social worker. At that time the public and professional perception and belief about hospices was that they were institutions for terminal care. I often visited clients in my local hospice, as well as in hospices in Brighton, and it was that early experience that prepared me emotionally and mentally for some of the challenges in palliative care social work.

The World Health Organisation (WHO) has defined palliative care as: 'an approach to care that improves the quality of life of people and their families facing the problems associated with life threatening illness, through the prevention and relief of suffering by means of early identification and impeccable assessment and treatment of pain and other problems, physical, psychosocial, and spiritual'. From my own experience and my role at the hospice, it is also a multi-professional service which provides holistic care for patients with a view to maximising their quality of life.

When I started at the hospice, my predecessor had left several months before. Consequently, I had to navigate my way around it alone, including planning and arranging my own induction. The medical and nursing team was enormously supportive of me during that period. The multi-disciplinary team at the hospice included doctors, nurses, a physiotherapist, a chaplain, a social worker, several volunteers, bereavement counsellors and many others. What was important within our multi-disciplinary, multi-professional unit was the respect we had for each other's disciplines and contributions. Having spent years working in the community and experiencing difficulties at times contacting and communicating with patients' doctors, here at the hospice, it was a refreshingly new experience to be working with doctors as part of a team and where there were no professional hierarchies in our working relationships.

Patients were admitted for one of three reasons: symptom control, short-term respite or terminal care. Of the three, not many patients were admitted for terminal care, which was contrary to my earlier belief that these were places where patients went to die. I found that after a short admission, most patients were discharged home. Patients and their families or carers were referred by the nursing staff to the social worker for a holistic social care assessment. This was an important part of the hospice discharge planning process, and my role was an important one with entailed social care assessments and liaisons with other professionals. From talking to patients and families, it became clear to me that for the most part, the patients wanted to spend their final days in their own homes, surrounded by their families. I was able to make this wish possible for many families.

A typical day for me began with a visit to the ward for an update from the nursing staff. Even though the written form I received contained information about the patient's diagnosis, condition and next of kin, it was always important to check with the nursing staff prior to any initial visit because the patient's condition could have changed after the referral was sent. I also needed to check what the patient understood about my intervention and that they had consented to the referral.

The initial difficulty I experienced when I started making my assessment visits was how to initiate conversation with someone who had a terminal or life limiting diagnosis. It was inappropriate to assume that the patient I was seeing had a thorough knowledge of his or her condition and prognosis. Neither could I assume that he or she knew the extent of my knowledge of these.

Another difficulty was the language and medical terminology of palliative care. As my grasp of these improved, so did my confidence in dealing with health professionals and patients. It was a revelation that some patients avoided the word 'cancer' when talking about their medical condition and preferred phrases like 'this thing' or 'it'.

I found that my traditional social work skills of listening and empathy were vital assets when faced with difficult discussions and assessments. Although the patients were admitted for symptom management or medical treatment, their medical condition often had a social impact which required my intervention and approach, for example, managing financial affairs, welfare benefits, liaison with Adult Social Care and solicitors, or simply providing emotional and psychological support to the family at difficult times in their lives. The psycho-social model and perspective of social work was valued by colleagues and complemented their medical model and perspective. As a multidisciplinary team we brought a holistic approach to patient care, treatment and assessment which incorporated the family, the community and cultural perspectives.

I spent a lot of time chatting with and listening to patients, their families and carers during the course of my assessments, and my overall experience was that most patients preferred to be cared for and to spend their final days at home, as long as high-quality care could be assured without placing too great a burden on their families and carers. I was particularly mindful of the key message from the national framework, which identified that social care had a vital role to play in supporting people to live and die well in the place of their choosing. I was conscious that Dame Cecily Saunders, founder of the hospice movement, had emphasised that 'how people die remains in the memories of those who live on'. After nearly ten years in various managerial roles, it was a soothing return to hands-on social work.

As a firm believer in the hospice movement and its underlying principal and philosophy, I was recently inspired by Rachel Clarke's memoir *Dear Life*, in which she recalled her experiences as a palliative care doctor. In a recent review of her book in *The Observer*, Dr Clarke talked about her meeting with Dame Cicely Saunders, not long before her death, and the assurance given by the Dame that the quality of palliative care meant that nobody needs to die in pain.

Working in this area and having to deal with the issues of death and dying on a daily basis was very stressful at times. I recall talking to a terminally ill woman who wanted to know about funeral costs and who would pay for her funeral, as she did not have the funds to do so and her family were not in a financial position to help. Feeling emotional and inexperienced at the time, I used the euphemism 'State funeral' to indicate that the public purse would pay if she and her family were unable. I remember her looking at me with a smile on her face and asking me if I was referring to a 'pauper's funeral'. I did attend a few of those funerals, and not only were there few people in attendance, there was also a social stigma attached.

Sitting next to a patient's bed listening to stories about their lives and their fears of dying could be very stressful. It could be very upsetting to learn that, after a great chat with a patient on a Friday afternoon, they had died over the weekend. Essentially the multidisciplinary team was very supportive.

Having lived and worked in East Sussex for most of my professional life, it was only to be expected that my hospice experience would include the dying and death of people I knew, including some former colleagues. The one which touched me the most happened during my first year at the hospice, when one of the patients was William, my first manager, the officer-in-charge at Old Roar House. I had memories of visiting his wife at the same hospice many years earlier and now he was dying in a room just along the corridor from my office. Other deaths touched me emotionally, including those of two young mothers, both in their early thirties, and the ensuing grief of their children and partners.

Working in a hospice environment where I was faced with the reality of terminal illness and mortality on a daily basis required effective support, including counselling and supervision. The hospice provided some, but as the lone social worker in a multi-disciplinary team I felt the need for external support. It was also important to maintain my links and contacts with social services and other agencies outside the hospice environment. I negotiated monthly supervisions and support meetings with a designated senior practitioner. I worked with the same practitioner to fast-track my assessments for packages of care for discharge planning. It was an effective relationship between two organisations that was beneficial to me as a social worker and to the patients at the hospice.

As a quid pro quo, I regularly invited social workers and social work students who were on placements to shadow me in order to gain experience and insight into palliative care and the role of social workers within the palliative care setting. I also welcomed social workers and students at our weekly multidisciplinary team meetings to gain the experience of seeing how inter-professional decisions are made. Alongside these, I also established and maintained similar useful networks with the Department of Work and Pensions, the housing authority and other welfare services.

My other important professional link was with the Association of Palliative Care Social Workers. Its mission was to raise the profile of palliative care social work within the profession and to provide support and disseminate literature and research. Regional meetings and conferences were held quarterly and hosted by one of the hospices within the region. I was proud to have hosted one of the regional conferences at the hospice where colleagues had the opportunity to tour the building. As this was in the summer, a walk to the seaside provided an additional bonus.

The association was a valuable network and a source of information about policy and training. The subject of death and dying in the twenty-first century raised many issues for professionals. These were often embedded in complex ethical, moral, religious, legal and medical debates. The association provided a forum for exploring these matters and for developing guidelines, such as a position paper on euthanasia, advanced directives and assisted dying. One observation of mine, made from attending the regional meetings, was that most of my social work colleagues had also come into palliative care work after many years of experience in social services or other statutory organisations.

While establishing myself and defining my social work role at the hospice, I had acquired a good knowledge and understanding of end-of-life and palliative care and had also identified gaps in social work education and training in the specialism. Similar gaps had been highlighted in the national framework. Chiming with my own assessment, the framework advocated the need to include end-of-life care in social work training. At the same time, academic papers and books were published specific to social workers in palliative care.

Furthering my passion for working with students, I used my contacts as a freelance lecturer at the University of Brighton to enhance the profile of the hospice by recommending it as a suitable placement for students. They established six-month placements and separately I was allocated two students at the hospice, who worked under my guidance and supervision as practice educator. After a successful placement, I was asked by the university to facilitate a series of workshops on end-of-life care and the issues and challenges for social work training and practice. Targeting social work students, as well as social workers studying for high awards, I ran the workshops for two years, and was encouraged by their positive feedback and feedback to the university.

Within my first few months at the hospice, I knew that I had made the right career move. On reflection, I was glad to have gone into this specialist area of palliative care social work towards the end of my career. I brought to it my experience of HIV/AIDS and the maturity of an experienced practitioner. Working there equipped me with confidence to deal with many of life's challenges, including death and dying. And apart from being the first Black social worker, there were no glass ceilings or invisible barriers preventing me from professional growth. The nursing and medical team were more culturally diverse than I had anticipated; we had doctors, nurses and other professional staff from different racial and cultural groups, which I found refreshing.

Unfortunately, that diversity was not reflected in the patients who were admitted to the hospice. From my experience, which is supported by what research seems to suggest, older Afro-Caribbean adults still adhere to the belief that 'there is no place like home' and therefore end-of-life care decisions are made with a significant emphasis on family structure and religion. Fortunately, that mindset is changing and patients from Black and minority ethnic backgrounds are beginning to access hospice care. The hospice also set up an at home service to help alleviate some of the burden on family members caring for their relatives at home. My hope is that the hospice will continue to be encouraged to promote this service, targeting Black and Minority Ethnic communities.

I became a grandfather for the third time during my fourth year at the hospice. A few years earlier, Karen had taken early retirement from her nursing career to assist our children and their families with childcare, and I felt that it was only fair for me to do likewise. I looked forward to spending more time with her and my grandchildren. I decided to explore the job-sharing policy in order to negotiate 'phase out' retirement by gradually reducing my hours. Another social worker who had taken study leave was lending her time to the hospice as a volunteer and agreed to take on the additional hours. After a year, I decided to formally notify the management of my desire to retire and my job-share colleague agreed to take the post on a full-time basis.

I cherished my six-and-a-half years with the hospice and was proud to receive my five-year service award. I am also proud of the contributions I had made to the hospice, not only in terms of direct patient care, but through my involvement in facilitating and safeguarding vulnerable adult-awareness training, policy development and education. It was an important time in my career, and even after my retirement and a few weeks' rest I found myself returning to the hospice on a volunteer basis, in day therapy, one morning a week, where I continue to enjoy the experience and the contact with patients and to contribute to their well-being.

CHAPTER 19

Training and consultancy

ONE OF THE AREAS IN WHICH I AM PROUD TO HAVE MADE A POSITIVE DIFFERENCE and to have raised awareness is in the approach to diversity in social work training and education, which has evolved through some significant changes and reorganisation in the sector. In this arena, training and consultancy, I feel I made the most valuable contribution to the social work profession. Prior to 1981, there was a gap in focusing on diversity issues. My specialisms enabled me to be successful in social work training and education, as did my role as mentor to other students, particularly BME students.

When I joined the local authority in 1981, social work students were required to demonstrate the ability to work within an anti-racist framework. Early in my career, I was drawn, perhaps for obvious reasons, towards race and diversity issues. Reflecting on those early years, I do not feel that the training we received really addressed the emerging cultural and racial diversity, something which I have already referred to in early chapters.

The training was good up to a point. I felt it was aimed at intervention with a white service user client group and Eurocentric in its emphasis. There were shortcomings in that it dealt with social class while failing to address core social work principles including social injustice, anti-oppressive practice, racism and other forms of discrimination experienced by many people. Having spent years in America, where those issues were being addressed at least a decade earlier than in the UK, as a Black practitioner, I recognised the gap in our social work training and education and felt the need to remedy that situation. This was another arena where there was a glass ceiling that I was determined to break.

The 1980s introduced a significant number of new legislations including the Mental Health Act (1983) and the Children Act (1989), with the next decade heralding the National Health Service and Community Care Act, (1990). A statutory requirement contained in all these legislations was the emphasis and statutory duty imposed on organisations and local authorities to recognise and take into account ethnicity in all assessments and for service providers to recognise and consider race and culture in any assessments of needs. These changes naturally had an impact on all future training and education. Unfortunately, in the absence of suitably qualified

internal trainers to prepare social workers for the implementation of these changes and legislations, senior managers took
on board the task of delivering race awareness training in a
tick-box manner. I became aware of this gap when I qualified
as a social worker, and now I decided to fill it.

I turned my focus to race and diversity training, where I
had identified a career level playing field in which I stood a
better chance of establishing myself in social services. I began
this journey by nominating myself for every available internal
or external training course relating to race and diversity.
My experience in the States had taught me that as a Black
professional I had to be above average in terms of qualifications
to be awarded even average consideration. Achieving that
necessitated a transfer from children services to adult services
where the opportunities were greater and more varied.

Having lived and studied in both Liberia and the States,
I had a good knowledge of the history and plight of Black
people in those countries, particularly African history and the
impact of colonialism. However, apart from insight into the
history of Windrush, when, in 1948, 492 passengers from
Jamaica arrived at Tilbury docks to begin a new life in the
UK, I had a more limited knowledge of Black British history.
I sought to remedy that by reading and researching the his-
torical role of Black people and colonialism in British society.
I hoped that this would put me in good position to impart
that knowledge to others, particularly social work students.
I was looking ahead to a future career as a freelance trainer.

The first opportunity to achieve that ambition came in

while studying for the Practice Teacher's Award, now referred to as Practice Educator's Award, at the University of Sussex. In October 2002 I was awarded the title of Visiting Tutorial Fellows in Social Work and Social Care by the Dean of the School of Cultural and Community studies, University of Sussex.

Achieving the Practice Teacher's qualification enabled me to supervise social work students on placements which was one way of raising my profile and visibility as a Black African professional. Towards the completion of the course, I was again approached by the university with a request to be a consultant to Black social work students. The university was trying to implement a recommendation made by a Black student in his MSc dissertation in which he recommended the introduction of a Black consultant who would act as a career role model, a person with whom Black students could meet regularly to share their experiences of racism. The specific rationale for requesting a Black consultant was that students would not have to retell their stories; the consultant would know where they were coming from and have empathy with their experiences.

I happily took on the role and began meeting regularly with the student, and within a month the university asked if I could include another student. In the same academic year, I was asked to work with three female Asian students who had heard about the service I was providing and had requested my support. In my meetings with the students, the Black and Asian women asked for advice and guidance on the application of empowerment theory. They shared the professional difficulties they had experienced when trying to empower their clients who in their private and domestic lives lacked power due to their gender.

One example remained in my mind for some time. It related to the fact that in their own home environment, the youngest male in the family would have his meal at the dining table before the women. The women were powerless to challenge this practice. I did some positive work with them by getting them to explore ways and strategies for speaking out against some patriarchal family traditions within the home. Some years later, I had the pleasure of working in the same team with one of the students, who was now qualified; she commented that my advice had helped her change certain behaviours at home.

The consultancy role opened further doors for me at the university. I was selected to sit on recruitment interview panels for social work students, and this led to the beginning of my involvement in facilitating workshops on race matters.

Working in the hospital health team, I was nominated for the approved social work training. Holders of this qualification are now referred to as approved mental health professional or AMP. Completion of the ASW, as it was then known, enabled me to undertake mental health assessments under the Mental Health Act, and to work more effectively alongside doctors and psychiatrists. Although the working partnership was both challenging and enjoyable, I felt that the doctors and psychiatrists had more authority in their assessments and diagnoses and that in reality this was not an equal partnership. This was easy to explain: my ASW training was more focused on the legal aspects of mental health than diagnosis and treatment. Nevertheless, I enjoyed working in the multidisciplinary team, yet I did feel a little envious working alongside doctors and psychiatrists who had a greater knowledge of the diagnosis and treatment of mental illnesses. I wanted to acquire similar knowledge.

With the encouragement of my manager and the approval of social services, I applied to the University of London to pursue the two-year part-time MSc in Mental Health Social Work based at the Maudsley Hospital in London. I combined this with the Advanced Award in Social Work (AASW) qualification.

The 1980s and early 1990s saw an increase in research literature on the mental health of minority ethnic groups. While some of these studies were informative, like the Harrison study in Camberwell, London, which focused on severe mental disorder in Afro-Caribbean patients and took account of social and demographic factors, others merely suggested that the rate of severe mental illness was highest among migrant groups in the UK. These studies were controversial, having failed to take account of other factors associated with the migratory process. Some authors began to look at the issue of racism in psychiatry.

I was always conscious of racism in psychiatry, particularly in diagnosis and treatment. As a descendent of freed Black American slaves, I was aware of the term 'drapetomania', used in 1851 by the American physician Samuel Cartwright to describe a category of mental illness that caused Black slaves to want to flee from captivity. It manifests itself by an unrestrainable propensity to run away. In his evidence to support his diagnosis, he pointed out that the Bible called for a slave to be submissive to his master. Closer to home, the phrase 'ganja psychosis' was a label and diagnosis applied to Black Caribbeans because of their addictive cannabis behaviour, yet not to white men who had the same addictive behaviour. Ethnicity and mental illness became my academic area of interest and formed the focus for my dissertation.

My professional interest in transcultural psychiatry began when I was assessing a patient for detention under the Mental Health Act. The patient was a doctor from Africa who was working in the UK. He had been assessed by the psychiatrist as having a mental disorder and being a risk to himself and his family. In retrospect I felt that there were cultural issues and factors which we, the professionals involved at the time, failed to consider in arriving at a diagnosis and course of action. I had a lot of empathy for this patient and felt that there were probably some cultural factors associated with his behaviour which we were unable and unqualified to recognise.

My proudest achievement in training and consultancy in race matters has to be my input and collaboration in setting up a consultancy group in 1997 to produce a video and training manual on race. The group consisted of Black and ethnic minority trainers drawn from across Sussex. Working alongside representatives from statutory services and local councils, we produced a training manual and DVD entitled *Race, It's Not An Issue Here*. Our aim was to help organisations promote and develop services for Black and minority ethnic individuals and groups and to raise awareness of key issues relating to race so as to provide statutory organisations with a framework for action. The training package was also intended to promote equal access and delivery of services in those areas where race and culture had not been perceived as being significant.

Following the production of the video and training manual, another collaborator and I formed a freelance training partnership and won a contract with the University of Sussex to facilitate workshops on race awareness for social work students. We identified the aims we wanted to achieve which included a review of the legal and statutory framework on race issues in the UK, institutional racism and its impact on service delivery, strategies for challenging racism and racial stereotypes, and how social workers and their organisations should develop a framework for improving performance on race matters.

The workshops were fully supported by the university and positively evaluated by the students. After two years my colleague decided to resume her doctorate. With the confidence I had acquired and my enthusiasm for the workshops, I continued to facilitate them alone, obtaining the same positive feedback. This was the beginning of my long visiting lecturer and consultancy relationship with the University of Sussex.

As the word spread of what the University of Sussex had initiated, I was approached by the University of Brighton to facilitate similar workshops on anti-racist social work. My involvement with Brighton continued for a longer period and led to further workshops, including some on race and mental health, asylum and immigration, the Equality Act and palliative care social work. Once again, the topics were well supported by the university and positively evaluated by the students involved.

The only difficulty I had in planning and delivering these workshops had to do with my availability. I was still a full-time employee with social services and I had to use annual leave days to run the workshops. Looking back, it was worthwhile and I have no regrets.

Momentum is an award-winning Black and minority ethnic mentoring scheme originally set up by the University of Brighton to pair BME students who wished to build confidence, gain employability skills and grow personally, with BME professionals who were willing to share their experiences. After my retirement from the hospice, I was invited to be the guest speaker at Momentum's annual award ceremony in 2015. I spoke about my journey as a Black professional and the value of education. Following this ceremony, I was asked to join the BME mentoring scheme for Black students. I am still involved in this scheme to this day and have successfully mentored two Black students. Following the positive feedback to the coordinator of the programme from one of my mentees, I was awarded a certificate as an acknowledgement of my work and commitment to the programme.

Finally, after thirty years, I retired as a practice educator at the end of the 2018 academic year. I wanted to do so on a high note and to reflect positively on the rewarding experiences I had enjoyed over my time. I worked one-to-one with over 50 social work students, not only from the universities of Sussex and Brighton, but also from the Open University, Royal Holloway and South Bank University in London. The thank you cards and appreciation I received from the students remain cherished souvenirs. It was an honour to observe the social work career progressions of many of my former students. Training and consultancy provided more of a level playing field than social work and created the opportunity for me – and for them subsequently – to make even larger cracks in the glass ceiling.

PART 7

THE BLACK PROFESSIONAL

CHAPTER 20

My quest for role models

UNDER SEVEN PER CENT OF THE POPULATION OF HASTINGS is categorised as non-white and less than two per cent as all Black or Black British. The proportion of non-white and Black people would have been significantly lower when I was employed with social services there. Prior to the murder in London of the Black teenager Stephen Lawrence in 1993, and the Macpherson Report's recommendations six years later, it was not a requirement by social services to specify race or ethnicity on applications for employment, so it is difficult to obtain accurate demographic data and figures for that time. Consequently, I came into a profession where there were no Black trailblazers, mentors or role models; no Black social worker from whom I could learn or whose experiences I could draw on. I was conscious of my ethnicity and the fact that I was beginning a career in a majority white organisation. Because my Blackness is a core part of my identity and defines who I am, my dilemma was how I would maintain that identity in such an environment.

In Chapter 1, I talked about Father Patrick as my first Liberian mentor and someone who inspired me. One of the Liberians he always talked about was Angie Elizabeth Brooks, the first Liberian woman and African to break many national and international glass ceilings. Among Ms Brooks' many achievements were that she was Liberia's first female Supreme Court judge and Liberia's permanent representative to the United Nations. In 1969, she was the first woman and African to be elected president of the UN General Assembly.

I had the pleasure of meeting this great Liberian and mentor in the early 1970 when, as president of the 24th session of the UN general assembly, she made an official visit to Grand Rapids, Michigan, where I was living and studying. As one of the few Liberians in Grand Rapids, I was invited to be on her welcome committee and had the opportunity to spend a few minutes alone with Ms Brooks before she went into the auditorium to deliver a speech on 'critical issues before the UN'.

Reflecting on my continuing quest for positive role models and mentors, I remember our son, Michael, who was then in primary school, saying to me after school one afternoon that his friends thought I looked like Trevor McDonald, the famous news reader and one of the few Black faces on national television in the 1980s. In his white friends' eyes this may have been a compliment, despite the fact that Trevor McDonald is much older than me and already had grey hair at the time!

That year I had the privilege of being guest speaker on Africa and Black British history at a local secondary school. I began my talk with an icebreaker by asking the students to name any famous Black man or Black woman in England. The outcome of the exercise was interesting, but not a surprise as an overwhelming number of the students responded with the names of popular Black sportsmen, sportswomen and musicians. To them the names were of Black people who were seen regularly on television and represented positive images of Black people. I attempted to balance the exercise by introducing the names of Black Members of Parliament and civil rights activists, but the names did not resonate with them.

There were a few Black students in the group and at that age where peer group acceptance and conformity are important, I wondered who those young pupils regarded as their role models or whether, as I experienced in boarding school, they had been told that all Black people were naturally good athletes or musicians. Research at the time suggested that the lack of strong male role models with whom Black teenage boys could identify was one of the reasons some were turning to more destructive ways of achieving that important sense of manhood and identity.

Louise Tickle, the award-winning freelance journalist, who has written on issues relating to education and social affairs, published an article in 2007 in which she highlighted the success of the Reclaim project in Manchester and its work with many inner city teenagers across the area and, in particular, the six-month project which targeted 49 Black boys between the ages of 12–14, from young offenders to high achievers. By involving a number of high-profile Black men, the project was aimed at getting the young boys to focus on aspirational Black male role models.

The majority white environment in East Sussex social services meant that there was an absence of other Black social workers or aspirational managers; consequently there were no role models or mentors for me to emulate or who might inspire and motivate me, particularly in the formative stages of my career. My awareness of this triggered a desire in me to become a trailblazer and role model to future Black workers joining the local authority after me.

My desire for a Black mentor and role model did not imply that there were not white colleagues and managers that I admired and who had a positive influence on my career. What I was searching for was a role model who had faced invisible racial barriers and had collided with the glass ceiling during their career and, therefore, could guide me on my career path. To achieve this I had to create opportunities rather than to wait for them to be created for me.

In contrast with social services, the hospital team in which I worked included a higher percentage of ethnic minority professionals, Black and Asian doctors and nurses. These health professionals seemed to have broken through the invisible barriers on their career journeys. I really admired that. However, on a closer assessment, it seemed that none of these was interested in being a role model or mentor to junior staff from ethnic minorities.

Little did I realise or anticipate that the first opportunity in my journey to becoming a mentor would not be to Black social care workers but instead to Black children in the care of the local authority. At that time I was unaware of the large number of West African children in private foster care with white carers in the area. Social services had become involved with some of these placements because of problems which had arisen with the private arrangements. Although the presenting problems were financial and behavioural, there were other problems associated with emotional insecurity and the lack of positive Black role models. Most of these private carers, despite good intentions, had a colour-blind approach to the welfare of Black children, believing that all children had the same needs and therefore could be treated the same. As a consequence the children were raised in an environment where they were unconscious of their ethnicity and were not equipped to cope with racism in their schools or in the wider community.

As a way of responding to the neglected needs of these children by supporting them and their carers, I was asked to work with them as a sessional worker, usually at weekends. My aim and focus were to give them a sense of identity and belonging and to work with their carers on how to recognise and provide for their racial needs and identity. During my time as a sessional worker I had the pleasure of working with many foster carers and more than ten foster children. I also worked with a few biological parents and succeeded in facilitating contact and rehabilitation where previous attempts had been unsuccessful.

A case which presented me with a particular emotional challenge was that of a teenage Nigerian girl who had been placed at a young age with private carers. Her parents then disappeared without leaving the carer any contact details. This young Black girl had an identity problem and believed that she was white. I found that with Black children in foster care their difficulties and behavioural problems are often attributed by professionals to problems of race instead of the developmental stage of the teenager. When the foster placement broke down because of 'behavioural problems' the girl was admitted to Old Roar House, where I continued to work with her. The teenage years are regarded as difficult and challenging for most young people and their parents or carers. For this teenager with the added problem of not accepting her racial identity, those problems were compounded.

Despite the fact that she was of a darker complexion than me she nevertheless was always saying to me that I was darker than she was and that her grandparents were white. The Home Office was also involved in her case and managed to trace her unknown grandparents, who consented to her return to them in Nigeria. I often wondered how she coped with the cultural shock of leaving the security of where she was to travel to a country she did not know and into the care of relatives she had never met.

After a few years in this additional role with Black children, other things began to happen. Social work students in the late 1980s and early 1990s were required by their universities to demonstrate a number of competencies, including working with minority ethnic groups during their placements. It took a while for the penny to drop and realise why so many students had started to contact me requesting interviews and discussions. It seemed that in the absence of having Black clients to demonstrate a competency and tick the box, a discussion and an interview with me would suffice. I went along with this for a while and then decided against the idea, simply because I was not a Black client. Students were getting the wrong impression: they were not interviewing white social workers to know what it was like working with white clients. They were not demonstrating competency in working with clients from ethnic minority groups.

In 1995, the video consultancy group on *Race: It's Not An Issue Here* brought together many Black professionals from across Sussex and in the process, created a powerful and enduring network of professionals who shared common experiences of personal and institutional racism. It was a great learning experience for all of us over the months we worked together. The highlight of those months was the honour and privilege of working with a person whose life and career as a Black man was a positive example and inspiration to us: Sir Herman Ouseley, Chief Executive of the Commission For Racial Equality. He gave the introduction to the video and provided the voice over.

Gratifying as it was being a mentor and source of support to others, my need for my own mentor and role model was not being met within social services. It was not until I began my academic journey that I found what I desired. I had the opportunity of meeting with two West African professors who not only inspired me by their achievements but also whom I regarded as positive Black role models and mentors. I was also moved by the work and life of Paul Stevenson, a Black social worker who lived in Bristol, and his continued campaigning against the exclusion of Black people from public places; in 1964 he had refused to leave a pub that refused to serve Black people. His campaign was strongly supported by local and national politicians, including Prime Minister Harold Wilson, who introduced laws against racism. In 1965 the first Race Relations Act was passed.

While studying at the Maudsley Hospital in London, I could not avoid noticing the number of Black domestic cleaners in the building each morning. As one of two Black students in my year group, I often wondered what the cleaners, who were mostly women, thought of us in that academic environment. Occasionally I stopped to have a social chat with them on my way to a lecture room. They seemed pleased that I took the time to do that, and I came away feeling that they were proud to see a Black person studying at an advanced level.

On the academic side, I was particularly pleased to see a large number of Black professors, including one who became my mentor and role model, Professor Eleanor Cole, who was born in Sierra Leone. As a woman and an African immigrant she had broken two glass ceilings and barriers on her academic journey. I treasured the informal conversations we had about West Africa and was impressed with her determination and success. I felt that if she could succeed as a Black woman in a white environment then so could I as a Black man aspiring to a masters' degree in mental health social work. In one of her lectures she revisited and summarised her research on 'pathways to care for patients with a first episode of psychosis: a comparison of ethnic minority groups'. I was impressed with the quality of her research and the relevance of her findings and conclusions to my understanding of mental health and ethnicity.

As a social worker, I often encountered racist abuse from clients but not in comparison to the abuse I encountered in the mental health team during assessments of patients under the Mental Health Act. It seemed that racist abuse was part of the territory for a Black person in my particular discipline. Unfortunately sharing one's feelings of racism and racist abuse with a white supervisor or colleague is not always easy. I benefited from my chats with the Black doctors and psychiatrists at the Maudsley, and from our shared experiences of racist abuse and strategies for dealing with it. Their advice and guidance gave me enormous confidence in dealing with unpleasant situations.

A few years after the successful completion of my studies at the Maudsley, I decided to study for my doctorate in social work at Brighton University. In the course of my study I encountered and was inspired by another West African professor,

Dr Kwame Akyeampong. Kwame, who was born in Ghana, was Professor of International Education and Development at the university. I was very proud to see another West African delivering a lecture to a predominantly white audience on 'The Power of the Case Study Method in Qualitative Research'. Once again, speaking with Kwame about Africa and his career I believed that if he could achieve what he had, then so could I.

As the new millennium approached the demographic profile of East Sussex social services began to change and to be a little more representative of the local population. Social work training and practice had gradually shifted to a race equality perspective where discussions about race was no longer an 'elephant in the room'. More Black social workers were seeking employment in the department and I begin to feel less isolated.

I was flattered but pleased that the induction programme for most of the Black intake had included advice for them to make contact with me, which most of them did. Together we formed a professional network in order to provide support to each other. This was very helpful in strengthening our resolve when dealing with the many invisible institutional barriers which existed. My role as their mentor and role model was regularly acknowledged and I reciprocated by informing them how helpful their presence and experiences had been to me.

CHAPTER 21

Race and the glass ceiling

'*I was taken aback when I found out I was the first Black female head of a university.*'

BARONESS AMOS

DISCUSSIONS ABOUT RACE AND THE GLASS CEILING ultimately raise questions about Black leadership and professional leadership prototypes. The question I pondered in the early stages of my social work career in East Sussex was how the glass ceiling impacted on Black professionals like myself. Could I reach leadership positions, particularly in an organisation where the cultural playing field was far from level and where being a Black professional often produced feelings of isolation and loneliness? I was aware that beyond outright discrimination, there would be psychological costs in becoming a leader or manager in an overwhelmingly white working environment.

Prior to my application for the job of operations manager, I knew that I had the necessary qualifications and the personal determination to break through the glass ceiling into that tier of management. As the first Black senior manager in East Sussex Social Services, I also knew that I brought something new to the organisation: added values of diversity of thought and of experience.

During that decision-making week, I came across an article by Derek Johnson in a popular social care magazine which resonated with my experiences and career journey. As chairman of the Association of Black Senior Managers, Johnson stated that before Black professionals can progress through the glass ceiling that exists within nearly every work place, they must first recognise that it is multi-layered and is constantly being repaired by those who wish to keep it in place. Once one Black individual breaks through, the ceiling closes in behind them, preventing others from getting through. I recognised this from my own experiences and challenged myself to prevent the local authority keeping out BME applicants.

The prevailing practice and culture which existed at the time was for most job vacancies to be filled by people already known to the interview panel. Managers on the panel tended to appoint candidates they perceived to be 'one of us'. I retain sad memories of my first unsuccessful application for the deputy principal post at Old Roar House when, during the interview, I was asked what the issues would be for me having to manage an all-white staff team. My experience of not being 'one of us' in relation to that interview meant that I found myself among colleagues with whom I could never feel safe nor comfortable. I would never be embraced as 'one of us'. Not being 'one of us' was an invisible barrier simply because I was excluded from social networks and contacts and, fundamentally, I was not a white male.

In The *Guardian,* social care network, Roy Taylor and Yvonne Coghill described an event for BME senior managers from the NHS and social services. This was the first time BME managers had come together to share their experiences and identify barriers to gaining top jobs. They discussed ways of breaking through organisational systems, visible and invisible, which never seem to shift. Unsurprisingly, during my career journey, I had been frustrated by two of the barriers that were highlighted: panel members appointing in their own image and having less access to significant networking opportunities.

There were two issues relating to the glass ceiling and Black professionals which I felt that unique meeting failed to address: unconscious bias and leadership stereotypes. Unconscious biases are social stereotypes about certain groups that individuals form outside their own conscious awareness. These automatic responses are triggered by our brains making instant judgements and assessments of people and are influenced by our background, cultural environment and personal experience. Unconscious bias can often lead to conscious action. In his book *Racism at Work: The Danger of Indifference*, Binna Kandola states that while most of us are not overtly racist, we all have unconscious bias. In a predominantly white workplace, where all the managers are white, this leads to discrimination.

The second issue relates to leadership categorisation theory and leadership prototypes which seem to suggest what a leader should look like. A person who is leader of a group is thought to possess features shared by most of the group members. Following my interview, I could see that I did not share any of the significant features of the group. In an attempt for recognition and to gain acceptance from the group I had to demonstrate similarities, for instance making myself visible at all social services social events including Christmas or office parties, going to a particular pub immediately after work and becoming a member of a particular gym frequented by senior managers. At these social events and gatherings the general conversation usually centred on work, including negative discussion and gossip about colleagues. It was incredible to me the extent to which work-related issues were shared at these gatherings by managers who were meant to uphold confidentiality.

After a year of engaging in this, I concluded that it was not the career tactic I wanted to play or the pathway I wanted to follow. I preferred to separate my working life from my private life; on reflection my attendance at these events and activities did not seem genuine. I began to understand the thinking and views of some Black professionals who simply wanted to get on with the job and not be drawn into any prevailing social network.

Three significant Acts of Parliament introduced between 1983 and 1990 changed the way statutory service providers engaged with and consulted with their local communities, including BME communities: the Mental Health Act (1983); the Children Act, (1989), and National Health Service and Community Care Act (1990). A key requirement of these new legislations was the statutory duty they imposed on local authorities to consider race, religion and gender in any assessment of needs and when providing services. This was a major challenge to East Sussex Social Services, whose initial response was to organise a series of in-house strategy meetings to discuss the process of consultation, the new buzzword.

A common experience among Black professionals like me in predominantly white organisations is the experience of being thrust into the role of 'expert' on all Black and multi-cultural issues whereby our views and opinions are regarded as representative of all Black and minority communities. In my case, while there were advantages which I enjoyed and from which I benefited, there were disadvantages, and an awareness of my identity as a Black person. There was an expectation that I would endorse or go along with policies which tried to treat or regard all minorities as a monolithic group. There was also the personal danger and fear of being seen by your own community as having sold out.

During the in-house consultation phase, I was asked to sit on and contribute to every policy meeting to discuss and formulate strategies for engaging with BME communities. Not wanting to bite the hand that fed me, while still wanting to be seen as a team player, albeit a player lacking power and status, I felt unable to decline the invitations to attend these meetings. I was very aware that my presence represented a 'tick in the box' for social services to claim that they had consulted with the local BME community. At these meetings I frequently reiterated that although I did have views as a Black professional, they were not representative of the local population or any BME group.

It was also difficult to recognise my views and input in policy documents and practice guidelines, with the credit attributed to a senior manager. Subsequently, I attended the meetings and deliberately remained silent, observing the reactions and body language of others around the table who were anxious to hear my views but did not want to single me out and cause embarrassment to the group.

An advantage of being regarded as the 'Black expert' was the opportunity that position and role gave me to remain up-to-date on race matters and national policy issues; it gave me the courage, confidence and power to challenge some practices and stereotypes. Acquiring this expertise enabled me to empower service users, informing them of their legitimate rights and statutory entitlements, and how to use complaint procedures. This proved valuable years later in my work with destitute asylum seekers. My specialist knowledge also benefitted me, removing some of the invisible barriers to the glass ceiling. Furthermore, I was no longer competing with white colleagues from a position of disadvantage. They seemed content with my role and to use me as their source of information and advice.

Despite the advantages for me in being recognised as the 'Black expert', I felt they were outweighed by the numerous disadvantages, such as being pigeonholed. I could see that my other social work skills and contributions would become marginalised or ignored, or that I would not be asked to speak on issues beyond race or BME. Discussing this with other Black professionals showed that we have shared experiences of this dilemma. As a direct result, some Black professionals have failed to progress outside the 'race box' and, as a result, their careers never seemed to progress.

At a reunion of some of the Black trainers and colleagues with whom I collaborated on the *Race, It's Not An Issue Here* DVD and training manual, I was somewhat surprised that unlike me, most of them, after almost 20 years, seemed stuck in that specific area of training and work. I feel the message that this sends out is that Black professionals can only be knowledgeable about Black issues and have those as their glass ceiling or pigeonhole and consequently are unable to move sideways.

My frustrations and experiences of attending weekly funding panel meetings and the feeling of being under a professional microscope and subjected to comparatively greater analysis and scrutiny than my white colleagues in my funding applications were described in an earlier chapter. My memories of these panel meetings were of being frequently talked over by others. When a Black professional or manager is seen as successful, their achievements are often attributed to factors other than their decision-making or leadership skills, but when their team fails, it is seen as the fault of leadership and incompetence. Unlike overt racist behaviours and attitudes, which are blatant, there are other behaviours which are subtle and which may not be perceived as racist by those displaying them.

As service manager for HIV/AIDS and substance misuse services, I also had to attend weekly funding panel meetings with other managers in the health team where we would all be negotiating for funding for our service users. On one particular morning, I overhead one of the other service managers asking all the other managers if she could have a chat with them after the panel meeting. I was aware that the invitation was not extended to me and that I had been excluded, which meant that after the meeting I was the only manager exiting the room. A few days later, I was informed that she had a Black social worker in her team with whom she was having difficulties and wanted to seek advice from the other managers.

I raised this issue of my exclusion with the manager the following week. In her response, she indicated that she had not included me because she did not want to compromise me, 'obviously' as another Black person. I was both angry and disappointed that she had made a judgement about me being compromised by a situation simply on the basis of race. This reinforced my awareness of the issues that hold Black professionals back and it left me thinking that if I had been experiencing a difficulty with a white member of my team, I would be unable to seek advice from other managers for fear of compromising them.

Social work education and practice have always demonstrated pride in its core values and beliefs about equality and anti-discrimination practices. However, the particular issues and experiences that Black professionals encountered in the workplace were regarded as the 'elephant in the room' and were never discussed in any team meeting. It was seen as an issue for supervision. I recall a training workshop to prepare social care staff for the implementation of the NHS and Community Care Act. The agenda included the subject of means testing service users to determine their financial eligibility for community care services and the introduction of ethnic monitoring of those accessing social care services.

The staff seemed comfortable with the new requirement of having to ask vulnerable clients about their financial assets and savings, yet when it came to monitoring race and ethnicity, participants in the workshop expressed their discomfort at having to ask clients and service users about their ethnicity. It follows that the only safe forum I had for discussing race and sharing my feelings and experiences was my informal network with other Black colleagues.

In social services we had a supervision policy, an arrangement which required monthly meetings between supervisor and supervisee. Supervisors were held to account if these monthly sessions did not occur. Supervisees also had to prepare for these meetings, the aim and purpose of which was to ensure and facilitate the ongoing development of organisational knowledge, skills and values. Records were made of the meetings and signed by both parties. Effective supervision with your manager provided a 'safe' place to reflect on practice, professional development and learning opportunities. The supervisory relationship was intended to be based on honesty, openness, empathy and respect. Finding that my manager referred to both me and other Black people as 'coloured' did not inspire confidence.

There was a general issue for white managers in their supervisory relationship with Black professionals. Most were ill-equipped, lacking relevant experience, cultural awareness and training to have been effective in supporting Black professionals deal with the various manifestations of racism and racist behaviour, including racist jokes and stereotypes that we encountered. It was often suggested or assumed that we were either being too sensitive or that we had a chip on our shoulders about our race. Earlier in this book, I shared my experience of being subjected to racist abuse from a client and my manager's response to another colleague was that 'James was probably used to that'. When my manager dismissed my experience of racist abuse because I was 'used to it', I was left feeling even more isolated in an institutionally racist organisation.

East Sussex Social Services did have a few white managers who had a good grasp and awareness of the issues Black professionals had to deal with on a daily basis. For instance, I would single out my manager in the HIV/AIDS and substance misuse setting. He provided me with developmental opportunities which paved the way for me to break through the glass ceiling. That would not have happened had I remained in children services at the time. I had to find an unusually supportive individual manager for that to occur. One of my all-time favourite books, as mentioned earlier, is *Invisible Man* by Ralph Ellison, who wrote about some of the intellectual issues facing Black Americans in the early twentieth century. Despite their achievements, Ellison observed that Black Americans still lived in a society and culture in which they were socially invisible.

In writing this book, I have reflected on the changes which occurred during my twenty-five-year career. Not only have Black professionals increased this visibility, but numerous glass ceilings have been cracked, including gender, religion and disability. In terms of race, I feel proud to have been one of the trailblazers in the process.

In 2015, Baroness Amos cracked the glass ceiling when she became the first Black person to lead a university college: SOAS, the University of London. In an interview following the appointment, she spoke for many of us when she talked about the mixed emotions of making history and the fact that it had taken so long. Speaking of the challenges as the first Black person she said, 'I know you can never please everybody. There will be high expectations which I'm not necessarily going to be able to meet, but I do think it's an opportunity to think about these issues.'

I am a firm believer that the glass ceiling can be completely broken. However, to accomplish that, as I did during my career journey, requires a sense of purpose, determination and a belief in oneself. Having followed in my career footsteps, my daughter has taken a good swing at cracking the glass ceilings regarding race and gender in less than ten years. She hopefully will smash them all and live in a world where none exist. With education, communication and understanding, we are proof that yes, it can be done!

Chronology

1947

2 July. James Martin Johnson born in Buchanan, Liberia.

1952

Primary and elementary education. St. Peter Claver Catholic school, Buchanan, Liberia. First two years as a day pupil rather than a boarder.

1963

January. Transferred to Bassa High School, Buchanan, Liberia

16 September. Left Liberia for private boarding school in Hastings, South East England, UK.

1967

September. Enrolled at Hastings College of Further Education, to study 'A' levels towards pre-med qualification.

1969

April. Returned to Liberia to family home to make plans for continuing studies In the United States.

1970

January. Left Liberia for Grand Rapids, Michigan, USA. Enrolled at Calvin College, Grand Rapids as pre-medical student.

1971

21 August. Our wedding day. Married to Karen in Sunshine Chapel, Grand Rapids.

1974

June. Graduated BA, psychology. Calvin College.

September. Enrolled at Western Michigan University, for postgraduate studies in behavioural psychology.

1975

Karen and I Left America for Liberia.

1976

March. Liberia Electricity Corporation (LEC). Employed as counselling and guidance administrator within the personnel department.

7 April. Michael Konjay Johnson (our son) born in Buchanan.

1979

14 April. Major 'Rice Riot' in Monrovia. Beginning of social and political unrest in the country. General feeling of fear and insecurity.

1980

February. LEC, appointed Director of Personnel.

5 April. Michelle Marjay Johnson (our daughter) born in Monrovia, Liberia.

12 April. Military coup in Liberia led by Sergeant Doe. President Tolbert murdered in the Executive Mansion and most of his cabinet executed days later.

June. Karen and the children leave Liberia for, Hastings, England.

August: Resigned from LEC.

15 September. Left Liberia for England to join family in Hastings.

1981

10 September. East Sussex County County (ESCC), Social Services. Employed as assistant group worker, Tile Barn, Children Centre, Hastings.

1982

2 April. ESCC, Old Roar Children Centre, Appointed Group leader.

1986

24 January. Central Council for Education and Training in Social Work (CCETSW). Awarded certificate in social services (CSS), after two years part-time study.

Promoted to group leader, Outreach Team.

1989

Liberia. Outbreak of first civil war. 250,000 deaths.
July. Transferred from residential to field social work.

1990

University of Sussex. Completed two years part-time post graduate course in child protection.

1992

May. Hospital team, Hastings. Appointed HIV/AIDS specialist social worker.

1993

June. Hastings and Rother Black and Ethnic Minority Forum. Elected chair.

July. CCETSW, Practice Teacher's Award.

November. Seconded to University of Sussex as tutor, social work and social care, two days a week.

1995

Member. Video Consultancy Group *Race is not an issue here*.

August. Senior Practitioner. Hospital Assessment Team. University of Sussex. Qualified as an Approved Social Worker (ASW; mental health assessment).

1997

July: Seconded senior practitioner, county-wide, HIV/AIDS and substance misuse.

1999

24 March. Appointed Acting Service Manager, HIV/AIDS and substance misuse.

April. Liberia. Outbreak of second civil war.
September. Appointed Service Manager.

2000

April. King' College London, Institute of Psychiatry. Graduated MSc (merit), mental health social work.

2001

March. CCETSW. Awarded Advanced Award In Social Work (AASW).

April. Sussex Police. Co-facilitated street intervention training for several months on street intervention.

April. Appointed Practice Manager for county-wide Asylum Team.

November. Sussex police. Invited to be an independent advisor.

2002

October: University of Sussex. Awarded the title of Visiting Tutorial Fellows in social work by the Dean of cultural and community studies. Also nominated as consultant to BME social work students.

University of Brighton. Visiting tutorial began.

2003

October. University of Sussex. Offered a part-time study reading for the degree Doctor of Social Work, DSW.

1 November. University of Sussex. Two years external secondment, part-time, tutor social work.

2005

January. University of Brighton, visiting lecturer, social work and social care.

March. Local authority cabinet decision to disband the asylum team.

June. Learning Disability Services, countywide residential placement team. Appointed Practice Manager.

2007

Intermitted from DSW course.

July. Retired from Social services.

August. Employed as palliative care social worker, St Michael's Hospice, Hastings.

2008

July. University of Sussex. Awarded MA, Social Work Research and Evaluation.

2013

July. Retired from hospice.

2014

Liberia. Outbreak of Ebola virus: 11,200 reported deaths.

2020

Global. Outbreak of Covid-19 pandemic. Worldwide lockdown.

References

Books

- Bolby, John (1969, 1973, 1980). *Attachment and Loss*. Volume 1–3, London. Hogarth Press.

- Butcher, Tim (2011). *Chasing the Devil – One Foot Through Africa's Killing Fields*. London: Vantage Books.

- Dominelli, L. (2002). *Anti-Oppressive Social Work*. Basingstoke: Macmillan.

- East Sussex Social Services Department (1993). *HIV/ AIDS Policy and Practice Guidelines*.

- Kandola , B. (2018). *Racism at Work: The Danger of Indifferenc*e. Location: Pearn Kandola Publishing.

- Kübler-Ross, Elizabeth (1969) On Death and Dying. 1st ed. Basingstoke: Macmillan.

- Lawyers Committee for Human Rights (1986). Liberia: *A Promise Betrayed. A Report on Human Rights*. New York, USA.

- Macpherson, W. (1999). *The Stephen Lawrence Inquiry Report*. London, HMSO.

- Saunders, C. (1990) *Hospice and Palliative Care: an Interdisciplinary Approach*. Sevenoaks: Edward Arnold.

- Ellison, R. (1952) *Invisible Man*. New York: Random House Publishing.

Journals/periodicals

- Amos, Baroness (2015) interview, *The Observer*, 19 July.

- Community Cohesion Update, Hastings and St Leonards 2015, Hastings Borough Council.

- Clarke, Rachel (2020). 'The doctor and how we should treat the dying. The Observer', *New Review* 26/01/20, 20–1.

- East Sussex County Council (2011). Census – small area population and household estimates … in brief.

- Francis, J. (1997). 'Black pride', *Community Care*, 11–17 Septermber.

- Johnson, D. (1999). 'A little help from my friends', *Community Care*, 28 January–3 February.

- Kitz, D. & Braly, K. (1933). 'Racial stereotyping of one hundred college students', *Journal of Abnormal and Social Psychology*, 28, 280–90.

- Kundnani, Arun (2001). 'In a foreign land: the new popular racism', *Race and Class: A Journal for Black and Third World Liberation*, vol. 43, no 2, October –December.

- Ineichen, B. (1989). Afro-Caribbean and the incidence of schizophrenia: A review. New Community 15(3) 335-341

- Prochaska, XX and Diclemente, XX (1983). 'Stages of change model for social workers'. *Trans Theoretical Therapy*. Vol/no,etc?

- Tickle, L. (2007,) 'Role models for Black teenagers', Education, *Guardian*, 23 October.

Video

- Video Consultancy Group (1995) *Race: It's Not An Issue Here*. Lighthouse Media Ltd, Brighton.

Printed in Great Britain
by Amazon

64779352R00172